D0236871

04268083

NO-BAKE BAKING

Easy
OVEN-FREE
CAKES & TREATS

SHARON HEARNE-SMITH

PHOTOGRAPHY BY DONAL SKEHAN

Quercus

CONTENTS

INTRODUCTION

Who says you need an oven to make delicious cakes, pies, tarts, biscuits, slices, bars and other sweet treats? This book turns baking on its head, with over 100 ingenious recipes that take the oven out of the equation and instead make clever use of your fridge, freezer, food processor and microwave, plus other small kitchen appliances.

No-Bake Baking will get you thinking well and truly outside the baking box. Discover gorgeous cakes made of crepes or cookies; twists on classic refrigerator cakes like tiffin and rocky road; divine no-bake cheesecakes; cute ice-cream cupcakes; impressive frozen bombes; inventive tart cases and biscuit bases; even surprising creations from your sandwich toaster, slow cooker and bread machine.

Put aside all fears of collapsed cakes, burnt edges or soggy bottoms, as these easy-peasy no-bake recipes promise brilliant results every time and will lure even beginners into the kitchen. They're convenient too, transforming handy supermarket ingredients (such as marshmallows, popcorn, breakfast cereals and condensed milk) into unique goodies in next to no time. Even those recipes that involve several stages or take a bit of time to set or freeze can be prepared well in advance and broken down into bite-sized steps.

In other good news, these oven-free treats generally come with the added advantage of a longer shelf life than their 'best eaten on the day' baked counterparts. Some, such as ice-cream cakes, last for a few months in the freezer (if they don't get gobbled up long before then!). And while your cakes might be considered 'hot stuff', you and your kitchen will stay nice and cool without the additional heat of an oven, which is especially good if you're baking in summer or a hot climate (plus you get bonus points for saving energy). One final thumbs-up is that many of these recipes are suitable for coeliacs, vegans and those with a dairy intolerance, particularly in the Biscuits and Slices & Bars chapters.

Most of all, *No-Bake Baking* is about having fun in the kitchen. Kids will just love to get involved too. So unplug that oven, throw out those baking preconceptions and whisk yourself up into a no-bake frenzy!

NO-BAKE
BISCUITS

Sesame Snaps

Handy to keep in your bag for a sweet nibble on the run, these are incredibly easy to make so don't be scared by the mention of a sugar thermometer. If you don't have one, just watch the colour of the caramel: it will be a rich golden when ready, but don't let it get too dark or it will taste burnt. If you'd prefer freeform shapes, use a large baking sheet instead of a tin and simply snap into shards.

MAKES 30

Sunflower oil, for greasing

100g sesame seeds

250g caster sugar

½ tsp ground ginger (or ground cinnamon or cardamom instead)

ESSENTIAL KIT:

Baking tin (roughly 18cm × 25cm)

Sugar thermometer (if you have one)

1. Lightly grease the baking tin with oil and line with parchment paper, leaving 5cm excess hanging over the edges.

2. Toast the sesame seeds in a dry, wide frying pan over a medium heat, tossing until evenly golden. Remove and set aside.

3. Gently melt the sugar in a medium saucepan over a medium heat, occasionally swirling the pan but not stirring, until it turns amber in colour. This will take 15–20 minutes.

4. Add the toasted sesame seeds and ginger, swirling the pan to mix them in, and let it bubble until rich and golden in colour (and reading 160°C on a sugar thermometer if you have one).

5. Working fast before it sets, pour the mixture into the lined tin and tip it into the corners. Leave for about 2 minutes to set a little. Use a lightly oiled table knife to score the surface into 3 equal strips down the length and 10 across the width, making 30 rectangles, each about 2.5cm × 6cm. Leave to set for 15–20 minutes. Then lift out, peel the paper off and snap into pieces along the score lines.

6. Layer between parchment paper in an airtight container and store for 3–4 days in a dry cupboard.

For an added twist . . .

★ Substitute some of the sesame seeds with desiccated coconut, or use a mix of black and white sesame seeds.
★ Dip the bars half or fully in melted chocolate and allow to set.

Dressed-To-Impress Shortbread Sarnies

These gooey indulgences are filled with dulce de leche, a caramel spread that will have you eating directly from the pot. Chill it in the fridge beforehand to avoid it oozing too much. If you want all your biscuits decorated the same, just double up the quantity of the chocolate or coconut, depending on your preference.

MAKES 12

1 tbsp desiccated coconut

50g dark chocolate (at least 70% cocoa solids)

24 round shortbread biscuits

400g dulce de leche caramel, chilled

1. Line a large tray or baking sheet with parchment paper. Toast the coconut in a dry, wide frying pan over a gentle heat, tossing regularly until golden. Tip onto a small plate and set aside.

2. Snap the chocolate into a small heatproof bowl. Either melt in the microwave in 30-second blasts, stirring between each go, or over a pan of simmering water, shallow enough that the water doesn't touch the bowl. When melted, remove from the heat and leave to cool to body temperature.

3. Lay 12 of the biscuits on the baking sheet, bottom-side up. Spoon the dulce de leche caramel evenly into the centre of each. Lay another biscuit, bottom-side down, onto each one, gently pressing down to sandwich the filling and ooze it towards the edge.

4. Gently, without squeezing too much, roll the edges of six sandwiches in the toasted coconut, pressing so it sticks to the filling. Return to the tray as you go. Dip the remaining six sandwiches halfway into the melted chocolate, tilting the bowl if necessary. Lay flat on the tray as you go. Chill in the fridge for at least 30 minutes until the filling is firm and the chocolate set.

5. These will keep for a day or two in the fridge, layered between parchment paper in an airtight container.

For an added twist . . .

★ Instead of coconut, gently roll the edges in edible sprinkles or toasted chopped nuts. The chocolate-coated ones can also be sprinkled with either of these, before setting.

Hazelnut & Oat Cookies

The fact that these keep well for up to a whole week means they win hands down in any competition against their baked counterparts. They are delicious with a glass of milk or a steaming mug of tea or coffee, or go well with soft desserts like fruit fool or chocolate mousse.

MAKES 20

25g desiccated coconut

125g whole blanched hazelnuts, roughly chopped

1 × 400g can condensed milk

200g rolled oats

1 tsp vanilla extract

1. Cut a 50cm length of parchment paper, ready for later.

2. In two separate wide, dry frying pans, toast the coconut and hazelnuts over a gentle heat, tossing regularly, until golden. Remove both pans from the heat.

3. Meanwhile, bring the condensed milk just to the boil in a medium saucepan, then remove from the heat. Add 50g of the toasted hazelnuts to the mixture. Stir in the toasted coconut, oats and vanilla extract to give a firm mixture.

4. Spoon into a 30cm-long sausage shape in the centre of the parchment. Roll the paper up to wrap the mixture, shape into a neat sausage, retaining this length, and twist the paper ends to secure. Lift onto a tray and leave for 30–40 minutes to cool completely, then chill in the fridge for at least 3 hours to set firm.

5. Once set, finely chop the remaining hazelnuts and scatter them onto a large baking sheet. Unwrap the cookie sausage and roll it back and forth over the nuts until evenly coated. Use a sharp knife to trim the ends flat and then slice 20 biscuits, about 1.5cm thick.

6. Serve in a pretty pile on a cake stand or in neat overlapping rows on a long platter. These will keep for up to a week layered between parchment paper in an airtight container in the fridge.

For an added twist . . .

★ Substitute the hazelnuts with any other nuts such as cashews, pecans or almonds.

Apple, Cinnamon & Toffee Waffle Melts

These super-simple melts are a perfect recipe for kids to help with, as they involve nothing more than a quick bit of chopping, some enthusiastic stirring and then the satisfying spooning out. Dried apple rings are available from most good supermarkets or health-food stores. If you have trouble finding them or prefer another flavour, use 25g of raisins or chopped dried apricots in their place.

MAKES 8

2 toffee waffle biscuits
200g white chocolate
½ tsp ground cinnamon
4 dried apple rings, roughly chopped

1. Line a large tray or baking sheet with parchment paper.

2. Cut the waffle biscuits into 1cm-wide slices, then cut them in half across the middle. Set aside.

3. Snap the chocolate into a medium heatproof bowl. Either melt in the microwave in 30-second blasts, stirring between each go, or over a pan of simmering water, shallow enough that the water doesn't touch the bowl. When melted, remove from the heat and stir in the cinnamon, waffle pieces and dried apple pieces until evenly coated.

4. Drop a heaped tablespoonful of the mixture onto the lined tray, pressing down a little to give a 10cm-wide disc. Repeat with the rest of the mixture to make eight discs in total. Leave to cool for 10–15 minutes before chilling in the fridge for at least 30 minutes until set firm.

5. Any that have not been devoured will keep for up to a week layered between parchment paper in an airtight container in the fridge.

For an added twist . . .

★ For a Christmassy cookie, use milk or dark chocolate instead of white, and 6 glacé cherries instead of the dried apple.

Fruit & Nutcase Chocolate Biscuits

These foolproof little treats will have your friends and family thinking you've been slaving away in the kitchen for hours. In fact, they couldn't be quicker to make. The ginger adds a nice fieriness but you can omit if you prefer. If you want to give them as a gift or are just feeling naughty, you can completely coat the finished biscuits in white chocolate.

MAKES 12

100g milk chocolate

100g dark chocolate (at least 70% cocoa solids)

75g rich tea or digestive biscuits

50g whole almonds, finely chopped

50g raisins, finely chopped

25g sultanas, finely chopped

1 piece of stem ginger (from a jar), finely chopped, optional

1. Cut a 30cm length of parchment paper, ready for later.

2. Snap both chocolates into a medium heatproof bowl. Either melt in the microwave in 30-second blasts, stirring between each go, or over a pan of simmering water, shallow enough that the water doesn't touch the bowl. When melted, remove from the heat.

3. Break the biscuits into small chunks, adding to the melted chocolate as you go. Add the chopped nuts, fruits and stem ginger, if using, and stir until everything is evenly coated.

4. Spoon the mixture into an 18cm-long sausage shape in the centre of the parchment. Roll the paper up to wrap the mixture, shape it into a neat sausage of even thickness, retaining this length, and twist the paper ends to secure. Lift onto a tray and leave to cool for 30 minutes, before chilling in the fridge for 1–2 hours until set firm.

5. Unwrap and slice into 12 biscuits, about 1.5cm thick, using a knife dipped in hot water and then wiped. If it is too crumbly to slice, leave it to come to room temperature and then try cutting again for a cleaner finish.

For an added twist . . .

* Popping candy makes a fun and surprising addition. Add about 2 tablespoons to the melted chocolate with the dry ingredients.
* For a citrusy twist, add the finely grated zest of 1 orange to the melted chocolate with the dry ingredients.

Cashew Butter Bites

Cashew butter makes a delicious change from the usual peanut version; you'll find it in health-food stores and some supermarkets. This recipe uses both a smooth cashew butter and chopped cashews for melt-in-the-mouth biscuits with a crunch. They're very delicate so leave them in the freezer until just before serving.

MAKES 15

50g unsalted cashew nuts, finely chopped

25g unsalted butter

225g icing sugar

100g condensed milk

75g cashew butter

Seeds scraped from 1 vanilla pod

1. Choose a large baking sheet that will fit in the freezer and line with parchment paper.

2. Toast the chopped cashew nuts in a dry, wide frying pan on a medium heat until lightly golden, tossing occasionally. Tip onto a plate and set aside.

3. Melt the butter in a large saucepan on the hob or in a bowl in the microwave. Sift the icing sugar into the butter and add the condensed milk, cashew butter and vanilla seeds. Beat everything together to give a smooth, soft dough.

4. Divide the dough into 15 even pieces. Between the palms of your hands, roll each piece into a neat ball and flatten into a disc about 4cm wide. Gently press both sides of each disc into the toasted cashews and place in a single layer on the prepared tray. Cover with cling film and freeze for about 2 hours until set firm.

5. Once frozen solid, they can be layered between parchment paper in a lidded container or freezer bag, returned to the freezer (for up to a few months) and removed when required.

6. Remove from the freezer only 10–15 minutes before serving as they defrost and soften quickly. Arrange on a cake stand to serve.

For an added twist . . .

* Before pressing into the chopped nuts, try half-dipping in melted chocolate for a naughty twist! Scatter the nuts over the chocolate and freeze as above.

Flash Florentines

These are flash in two senses of the word: speedy *and* impressive! They are a great way to use up leftover nuts and dried fruits; substitute those in the recipe with the same weight of any others you prefer. These make a beautiful gift in a cellophane bag or glass jar, tied with ribbon and a pretty tag.

MAKES 15

50g unsalted butter

100g caster sugar

100g soft light brown sugar

50g crème fraîche

1 piece of stem ginger (from a jar), finely chopped

150g flaked almonds

50g dried cranberries

50g mixed peel

1 tsp vanilla extract

¼ tsp bicarbonate of soda

50g dark chocolate (at least 70% cocoa solids)

1. Line a large baking sheet with parchment paper and set aside. Melt the butter in a medium pan over a low heat. Add both sugars, turn the heat up high and stir for 4–5 minutes until smooth and gooey.

2. Carefully stir in the crème fraîche, as it may spit. It will cause the sugar to harden but just continue stirring over a high heat until dissolved again. Then leave to bubble away for 3–4 minutes, stirring occasionally, until reduced and thickened.

3. Remove the mixture from the heat and stir in the chopped stem ginger, almonds, cranberries, mixed peel, vanilla extract and bicarbonate of soda.

4. Drop 15 heaped tablespoons of mixture onto the lined baking sheet, flattening into round discs about 6cm wide. Leave to cool for 10–15 minutes then chill in the fridge for about 30 minutes to set firm.

5. When the Florentines are set, snap the chocolate into a small heatproof bowl. Either melt in the microwave in 30-second blasts, stirring between each go, or over a pan of simmering water, shallow enough that the water doesn't touch the bowl. When melted, remove from the heat and leave to cool to body temperature.

6. Once cool, spread about ½ teaspoon of melted chocolate onto the bottom of a Florentine and pop it back on the tray, chocolate side down. Or place on a wire rack so excess chocolate can drip off. Repeat with the remaining biscuits and chocolate, and put in the fridge for 15 minutes to set.

7. These are now ready to enjoy or will keep for 2–3 days, layered between parchment paper in an airtight container in the fridge.

Chewy Toffee & Salted Cashew Cookies

These cute little cookies have only 4 ingredients and can be prepared in about 4 minutes! They can also be made into fingers by pressing the mixture into a parchment-lined 450g loaf tin (about 10cm x 20cm) and leaving to set before cutting into 16 bars.

MAKES 22

250g individually wrapped toffee sweets

2 tbsp double cream

1 tsp vanilla extract

300g salted cashew nuts

1. Cut a 40cm length of parchment paper, ready for later.

2. Unwrap the toffees and place in a medium saucepan with the cream and vanilla extract. Warm through on a gentle heat, stirring constantly, until the toffees have completely melted into a thick toffee sauce. Remove from the heat and stir in the cashew nuts until completely coated.

3. Working quickly, spread the mixture out with the back of a spoon into a long sausage shape (about 22cm) in the centre of the parchment. Wearing rubber gloves to protect your hands from the heat, roll the paper up to wrap the mixture, massage it into a neat sausage shape, retaining this length, and twist the paper ends to secure. Lift onto a tray and leave to cool for about 30 minutes, before chilling in the fridge for at least 1 hour until set firm.

4. Once set, peel the paper away and use a sharp knife to cut into 22 slices about 1cm wide.

5. Serve in a pretty pile in a paper-lined tin or on a cake stand or in neat overlapping rows on a long platter. Store for 3–4 days, layered between parchment paper in an airtight container in the fridge.

Build Your Own S'mores

You'll love these sandwiches of warm gooey marshmallow squished between chewy cookies and laced with delicious sauces and sprinkles. They are so much fun to serve at a party and you can load the tray with any fillings you like and let your guests create their own combinations. The marshmallows are of course great toasted on a barbecue or campfire – hold them over the heat on sticks or skewers and then slide them carefully onto the cookies.

SERVES 6

250ml Chocolate Sauce (page 183)

125ml Heavenly Caramel Sauce (page 182)

100g pecan or hazelnut Praline (page 183), optional

2 tbsp desiccated coconut

125g fresh raspberries

2 tsp edible sprinkles

12 large chocolate chip cookies

150g marshmallows

1. Prepare a 'build your own s'mores' tray with six small serving bowls, six teaspoons and six napkins or parchment pieces.

2. If you haven't already done so, make the chocolate sauce, caramel sauce and praline (if using), and spoon into three of the bowls.

3. Toast the coconut in a dry, wide frying pan over a medium heat, tossing until golden. Spoon into another bowl on the tray to cool.

4. Crush the raspberries with a fork to release their juices and spoon into another small bowl. Toss the edible sprinkles into the remaining bowl. Finally, nestle six of the cookies onto the tray.

5. When ready to serve, turn the grill on to a high heat and place the shelf in the middle. Arrange the six remaining cookies bottom-side up on a baking tray and divide the marshmallows evenly between them in a single layer. Place under the grill for about 1 minute, keeping your eye on them as the marshmallow may burn quickly, until slightly charred and beginning to soften and ooze. Don't be tempted to touch the marshmallow at this stage as it will be extremely hot. Carefully remove the biscuits from the grill and leave to cool for a minute or two.

6. Invite everyone to take a marshmallow cookie on a piece of parchment paper or napkin from the tray. Then they can help themselves by spooning their choice of drizzles, dollops, sprinkles and sprozzles over to make their own bespoke s'more, sandwiched with another cookie from the tray.

Peanut Butter & Banana Flying Saucers

These are like cookies crossed with cake. As if that's not tempting enough, they are ready quicker than you can say 'flying saucer', using your microwave as a sneaky alternative to the oven. They are best cooked to order and eaten straight away. The mix can be made a few hours ahead and kept in the fridge if you want, but it is so quick to make that it won't take long to do it all in one go.

MAKES 2

2 tbsp unsalted butter

2 tbsp smooth peanut butter

6 tbsp plain flour

2 tbsp soft dark brown sugar

2 tbsp maple syrup

½ banana, mashed

2 egg yolks

¼ tsp ground cinnamon

75ml thick cream or crème fraîche, to serve

ESSENTIAL KIT:

2 microwave-proof saucers (or side plates), at least 15cm wide

Microwave

1. Melt the butter and peanut butter together in a medium bowl in the microwave. Add all the other ingredients except the cream or crème fraîche, and stir until well mixed. Spoon the mixture evenly between the two saucers or side plates.

2. Microwave on high (900W) for 1½–2 minutes until cooked through. Leave to sit for a few minutes and then serve warm with a dollop of thick cream or crème fraîche.

For an added twist . . .

★ Peanut butter, apple and raisin flying saucers: Instead of the cinnamon and banana, add ¼ teaspoon of mixed spice, ½ a Granny Smith apple, roughly grated, and 1 tablespoon of roughly chopped raisins.

★ Peanut butter, ginger, lime and chilli flying saucers: Instead of the cinnamon and banana, add a 2cm piece of fresh ginger, peeled and finely grated, the finely grated zest of ½ a lime and ½ a red chilli, deseeded and finely chopped.

NO-BAKE
CAKES

Blackberry Swirl Marshmallow Gateau

Continental sponge flan cases are usually served filled with cream and fruit but here they're transformed into the layers of a gateau. Any 20cm cake can be used in the same way. The trimmings can be put towards the Giant Upside-Down Lollipop Cake (page 44) or one of the Jam Jar Gateaux variations (page 164). The marshmallow can also be made on its own. Leave it to set in a lined 18cm square tin, then cut into cubes and toss in icing sugar.

SERVES 8

2 × 200g continental sponge flan cases

Sunflower oil, for greasing

2 tbsp icing sugar

75g fresh blackberries

1 fresh mint sprig

150ml double cream, optional

125g Blackberry Purée (page 185)

BLACKBERRY COMPOTE:

125g fresh blackberries

2 tbsp caster sugar

MARSHMALLOW FILLING:

23g powdered gelatine (2 × 11.5g sachets)

450g caster sugar

150ml maple syrup

ESSENTIAL KIT:

20cm round, loose-bottomed cake tin

Food mixer

Sugar thermometer (if you have one)

Thin metal skewer

Gas hob or blowtorch

1. Turn the cake tin upside down and sit it onto one of the flan cases. Press down to stamp out a circle. Repeat with the second flan case. With a long, sharp knife, carefully slice each one in half horizontally, giving you four thin sponge discs. Set aside the best-looking one for the top. Reserve the trimmings for another use (see intro). Grease the sides of the cake tin with oil and line with parchment paper. Sit one of the sponge discs in the bottom.

2. To make the blackberry compote, place the blackberries in a small saucepan with the sugar. Crush roughly and cook over a medium heat for 1–2 minutes until soft and slightly thickened. Remove and leave to cool.

3. To make the marshmallow, pour 75ml of cold water into the bowl of a food mixer. Sprinkle in the gelatine and stir gently to ensure it's all soaked. Leave for 5–10 minutes until all the water is absorbed.

4. Meanwhile, put the caster sugar, maple syrup and 100ml of water in a small heavy-based saucepan and stir over a low heat until the sugar dissolves. Then turn up the heat, bring to the boil and leave to bubble gently until it reaches 130°C on a sugar thermometer (if you don't have one, you need the mixture to reach hard-ball stage – drop a tiny bit of mixture into a bowl of iced water and it should turn into a hard ball when rolled between your fingers). This takes 4–5 minutes and the syrup will become dark amber in colour. Remove immediately from the heat and leave to cool for 1 minute.

CONTINUED

⟹ *CONTINUED FROM OVERLEAF*

5. Once the gelatine has soaked up all its water, turn on the food mixer to a low speed to break it up a bit. Then slowly and carefully trickle in the warm syrup, down the inside of the bowl rather than onto the whisk. Once all the syrup is added, whisk for 2–3 minutes until the mixture grows in volume and becomes stiff and meringue-like. Fold in the blackberry compote with a spatula, gently rippling it rather than completely blending.

6. Working quickly, pour one-third of the mixture over the sponge base in the tin, levelling it with the back of a spoon. Lay another sponge disc on top, followed by another third of mixture, again levelling smooth. Add a third disc and the remaining filling, and finish with the final (best-looking!) sponge disc on top. Cover with cling film and leave to set for about 1 hour until firm when pressed. The gateau can be prepared to this stage up to 24 hours in advance. It doesn't need to be stored in the fridge, just keep it airtight.

7. When ready to serve, remove from the tin, peel off the paper, sit on a cake stand and dust the top evenly with icing sugar. Carefully heat the length of a thin metal skewer in the flame of a gas hob or blowtorch until searingly hot. Press the hot skewer onto the centre of the cake top to make a brand mark. (The smoke is nothing to worry about; it creates a bit of drama!) Continue to brand the top at 2.5cm intervals either side of this middle line, wiping and reheating the skewer each time before pressing it down. Then turn the cake 45 degrees and repeat the spaced markings. This creates a pretty diamond pattern.

8. Finally, arrange the whole blackberries in a neat pile on the cake and add the mint sprig. Softly whip the cream (if using) and serve along with the blackberry purée. Cut the cake into eight wedges.

Ginger Paradise Cake

Jamaican ginger cake is a classic on its own, but here its spicy flavour is brought well and truly to life with the addition of lime, coconut, mango and mint. It just screams the Caribbean! This cake is best assembled just before serving but everything can be prepared in advance.

SERVES 6–8

25g desiccated coconut

250g mascarpone

2 pieces of stem ginger (from a jar), finely chopped, reserving at least 1 tbsp of syrup

Finely grated zest and juice of 2 limes

175ml double cream

2 × 230g Jamaican ginger cakes

1 small ripe mango

Small handful of fresh mint sprigs

1. Toast the coconut in a wide, dry frying pan over a medium heat, tossing until golden brown. Tip onto a plate and leave to cool.

2. Place the mascarpone, chopped stem ginger (not the syrup), lime zest and juice in a large bowl and beat together until smooth. Softly whip the cream in another bowl, gently fold it into the mascarpone mixture and set aside.

3. Cut the ginger cakes horizontally in half to give four pieces in total. Lay one on a rectangular serving plate and spread a quarter of the mascarpone mixture evenly over it. Top with another layer of cake, followed by another quarter of filling. Repeat until all the cakes are used up and end with the mascarpone mixture on top.

4. Prepare the mango by slicing off the cheeks from each side of the stone. Cut each cheek in half lengthways and then peel by running your knife under the flesh close to the skin. Cut each of the four pieces into long thin strips. Toss the mango in a small bowl with the ginger syrup and arrange the slices across the top of the cake.

5. To finish, stick the toasted coconut onto the edges of the filling at the sides of the cake. Arrange the mint sprigs on top and serve. This can be cut into six or eight slices.

For an added twist . . .

* Use finely chopped nuts instead of coconut if you prefer.
* You can top with other tropical fruits like kiwi, pineapple, papaya or passionfruit.
* Drizzle Malibu over the cake layers for an extra tropical hit.

Turtleback Terrine

This terrine is so-called because the pattern made by the nuts and caramel sauce on top resembles a turtle shell. You can vary the nuts and even add dried fruits for a different turtleback every time.

SERVES 6

Sunflower oil, for the tin

CHOCOLATE LAYER:

400ml double cream

400g dark chocolate (at least 70% cocoa solids)

TOPPING:

250ml Salted Caramel Sauce (page 182)

75g pecan nuts

75g whole almonds

75g hazelnuts

ESSENTIAL KIT:

900g loaf tin (roughly 23cm × 10cm)

1. If you haven't already made the salted caramel sauce for the topping, do so and leave to cool to room temperature.

2. To prepare the chocolate layer, bring the cream gently to the boil in a medium pan on a medium heat. Meanwhile, snap the chocolate into a large jug. Remove the cream from the heat once it reaches the boil and pour over the chocolate. Stir until melted to a smooth, rich sauce, then leave to cool to body temperature. Meanwhile, oil the loaf tin and line with parchment paper.

3. Stir the nuts through the salted caramel sauce and then pour into the base of the tin, spreading it evenly with the back of a spoon. Pour the cooled chocolate mixture on top, cover with cling film and refrigerate for at least 4 hours or overnight, until set firm. This can be made up to 24 hours in advance and left in the fridge.

4. Just before you want to serve, lay a long serving board upside down over the tin and turn both over together, allowing the terrine to drop out. Remove the tin and peel off the paper to reveal the turtleback. Leave to come to room temperature for 15–20 minutes before serving. Dipping your knife in boiling water and wiping dry between every slice, cut into 12 slices, serving 2 per person.

For an added twist . . .

★ The chocolate layer can be flavoured with any of the following: finely grated zest of 1 orange or lime; a dash of brandy, Baileys or Amaretto; 2 tsp instant coffee; 125g fresh raspberries; a finely chopped red chilli; 1 tsp ground cinnamon.

★ Serve the chocolate layer alone by pouring into small espresso cups or pretty glasses. Set and serve with a crisp biscuit.

Rice Krispie Ruffle Cake

Under these stunning blue ruffles hides a delicious cake of crispy rice and edible pearls set in marshmallow. The frilly icing may look a little daunting but it doesn't take long to get the hang of it. Practise the first frill on the cake and keep removing it until you feel confident enough to go for the whole thing. All you need is a piping bag with a teardrop-shaped nozzle called a petal nozzle.

SERVES 20
(8 from top tier and 12 from bottom)

Sunflower oil, for greasing

125g unsalted butter

600g marshmallows

400g Rice Krispies

100g edible pearls

BUTTERCREAM ICING:

325g unsalted butter, softened

600g icing sugar

2 tsp vanilla extract

3 tbsp whole milk

Blue paste food colouring (avoid liquid colouring)

ESSENTIAL KIT:

15cm round, loose-bottomed cake tin, 8cm deep

20cm round, loose-bottomed cake tin, 8cm deep

Food mixer (if you have one)

Regular or disposable piping bag, fitted with a small petal nozzle

1. Grease both cake tins with oil, then line the base and sides with parchment paper.

2. Melt the butter for the cake in a large saucepan over a medium heat. Add the marshmallows and stir with a heatproof rubber spatula until melted. Tip in the Rice Krispies and 75g of the edible pearls and stir gently until well coated.

3. Working quickly before it sets, spoon the mixture into the two tins, pressing it down gently with the back of your spoon to compact it as you go. Fill them right to the top, levelling the mixture flat. Cover both with cling film and leave for 1 hour to cool and set firm – or until ready to use; they can be prepared up to 24 hours in advance.

4. Meanwhile, make the buttercream, which is easiest with an electric food mixer. Beat the softened butter in a large bowl until pale. Sift in the icing sugar and beat well to give a smooth mixture. Add the vanilla extract and milk and blend to loosen a little. Add the blue colouring a tiny bit at a time until you reach your preferred shade. The colour will intensify as the icing sits, particularly when out of the fridge. Cover and refrigerate for about 15 minutes to firm up a little. This can be prepared up to 24 hours in advance and left in the fridge, but it will harden, so remove it about 15 minutes before you need it to let it soften up.

5. When the cakes are set, carefully lift from the tins and remove the paper. Spread a couple of tablespoons of buttercream in the centre of a stand and stick down the larger cake. Then spread another

CONTINUED

⇨ *CONTINUED FROM OVERLEAF*

tablespoon of icing in the middle of the cake and stick the smaller cake well centred on top.

6. Spoon the remaining icing into the piping bag. Starting at the bottom of the larger cake, hold the piping bag vertical against the side of the cake with the wide end of the petal nozzle touching the cake and the thin end pointing outwards. Now pipe back and forth across a 1.5–2cm width, working upwards until you reach the top of this cake and firmly squeezing the bag as you go. That's one frill done, now repeat until the sides of both cakes are covered.

7. To ice the tops of the cakes, start from the outside and work inwards, with the bag held vertical and the fat end of the petal shape facing the centre, this time working the back and forth motion around the outer edge. Then pipe another circle inside and so on, until the tops are completely covered.

8. Finally, sprinkle with the remaining edible pearls and go wow your guests. The easiest way to cut this is to lift the top cake carefully onto a chopping board. Then cut into 8 wedges and the larger cake into 12 wedges, and serve.

Chocolate & Cardamom Cake-in-a-Cup

Made to order in an instant with the help of your microwave, this is a recipe to keep up your sleeve for times when you fancy a really quick but indulgent fix. The cooked cakes are best eaten straight away – not that you'll be able to resist anyhow! Don't worry if the chocolate topping starts to sink into the mixture – it will create a gooey chocolate centre. Simply halve the cake quantities if you're indulging all alone.

MAKES 2

4 tbsp self-raising flour

3 tbsp cocoa powder

½ tsp ground cardamom

4 tbsp soft light brown sugar

1 egg

5 tbsp hazelnut chocolate spread (such as Nutella)

3 tbsp sunflower oil

3 tbsp whole milk

½ tsp vanilla extract

50ml double cream

ESSENTIAL KIT:

2 × 250ml microwave-proof mugs

Microwave

1. Sift the flour, cocoa powder and cardamom into a medium bowl, stir in the sugar and make a well in the centre. Break in the egg, add 3 tablespoons of the chocolate spread, the oil, milk and vanilla extract and mix everything together really well to give a smooth, thick batter.

2. Divide evenly between the microwave-proof mugs and spoon a tablespoon of chocolate spread on top of each. Microwave on high (900W) for 1 minute and then carefully remove and leave to stand for a couple of minutes to finish off cooking in their own heat and to cool down a little.

3. Meanwhile, softly whip the cream in a small bowl.

4. The cake should now be cooked but still moist and a little gooey in the centre. Dollop the cream on top and enjoy straight away.

For an added twist . . .

★ Instead of chocolate spread, dollop a tablespoon of peanut butter or dulce de leche caramel into the cup before cooking. If using these alternatives, omit the cardamom.

★ This is also delicious with freshly grated orange zest instead of cardamom.

Strawberry Charlotte

A charlotte is a French cake in which sponge fingers form the sides, concealing a set fruit mousse filling. You can add chopped strawberries to the filling if you want more texture and colour throughout.

SERVES 8–10

200g caster sugar

Sunflower oil, for greasing

350g sponge fingers (about 60, depending on size)

FILLING:

8 gelatine leaves

400g Strawberry Purée (page 185)

100g caster sugar

325ml double cream

500g natural yoghurt or natural fromage frais

TO FINISH:

500g fresh strawberries, halved if large and with most green tops removed

Small handful of fresh mint sprigs

150ml double cream, softly whipped

ESSENTIAL KIT:

20cm round, springform cake tin

1. For the filling, soak the gelatine leaves in just enough cold water to cover, for 5–10 minutes until soft. Make the strawberry purée if you haven't yet, pour into a wide frying pan and simmer over a medium heat for about 5 minutes until reduced by half and thickened.

2. Meanwhile, place the sugar for the sponge fingers in a medium saucepan with 200ml of water and bring to the boil on a high heat, stirring until dissolved. Give it another minute before pouring into a wide baking dish. Leave the sugar syrup to cool slightly.

3. When the purée has reduced, stir in the filling sugar until dissolved, then remove from the heat. Squeeze excess water from the soft gelatine and stir into the purée until dissolved. Leave to cool.

4. Whip the cream in a large bowl until just stiff. Fold into the yoghurt or fromage frais in another large bowl until blended.

5. Grease the tin and line the sides with parchment. Soak a few biscuits at a time in the sugar syrup for 30–60 seconds, turning halfway, until softened but not soggy or breaking. Carefully place upright against the tin edge, sugared side outwards. You will need about 30. Soak half the remaining biscuits in the syrup and lay them flat in the tin, trimming to cover the base completely.

6. Gently fold the cooled purée into the cream mixture until well blended. Pour half into the tin and smooth with the back of a spoon. Soak the remaining biscuits in the syrup and arrange on top, trimming to fit. Pour the remaining filling over, smoothing again. Cover with cling film and chill for 3 hours or overnight until firm.

7. Carefully remove from the tin, place on a stand and peel away the paper. Decorate with strawberries and mint sprigs on top. Cut into wedges and serve with softly whipped cream.

Pinwheel Fairy Cakes

Here's a cute way to pimp up plain shop-bought fairy cakes with fondant icing. For the textured fondant disc, use an embossing mat or textured rolling pin, which can be bought from good baking supply stores or online – or improvise with something textured that you have at home. For a party, why not make both red/blue and green/white combinations. If you're feeling flashy, you can even make the icing striped, by assembling it from strips of alternate colours gently rolled together. The pinwheels are best left for a day or two so the icing dries out.

MAKES 12

200g blue (or green) ready-to-roll fondant icing

200g red (or white) ready-to-roll fondant icing

25ml vodka

50g white (or red) ready-to-roll fondant icing

12 shop-bought fairy cakes

Pearl white edible lustre dust, optional

BUTTERCREAM:

50g unsalted butter, softened

75g icing sugar

¼ tsp vanilla extract

ESSENTIAL KIT:

12 x 7.5cm lollipop sticks

5mm-wide plain piping nozzle

Embossing mat or embossing rolling pin, if you like

6cm round, fluted cutter

1. Line a large tray with parchment paper and set aside.

2. Roll out the blue icing on a sheet of parchment paper to a large rectangle about 3mm thick. Trim down to 15cm x 20cm, reroll the trimmings and wrap well. Repeat with the red icing. Wet a pastry brush with vodka and dampen the surface of one rectangle, then carefully stick the other directly on top. Cut the two-layer rectangle into twelve 5cm squares.

3. Work with one square at a time and cover the rest with cling film to prevent them drying out. Using a sharp knife, cut a 2cm incision in from each corner towards the centre. The cuts should not meet in the middle – instead dab this area with a tiny bit of vodka on your finger. Lift one corner, fold it into the centre and stick, then dab the top with vodka. Lift the matching corner of the next side along, fold that in and again dab with vodka. Repeat with the remaining two corners to create a pinwheel.

4. Repeat the previous step to make 12 pinwheels in total. Make both blue/red and red/blue combinations by alternating which colour is on top when you start folding. Arrange on the prepared tray as you go, then set aside.

5. Divide the white icing in half and roll one piece into a ball, keeping the other wrapped in cling film. Cut the ball into 12 equal pieces and roll each into a small ball (about 1.5cm diameter). Place one on top

CONTINUED ➧

⇒ *CONTINUED FROM OVERLEAF*

of each lollipop stick and squeeze slightly so it looks like a little hat on the stick. Dab vodka on one flattened side of this hat and then gently stick it to the back of a pinwheel. Lay it gently back on the tray.

6. Roll out the other piece of white icing, again on a sheet of parchment, to 2mm thick. Use the tip of the piping nozzle to stamp out around 100 tiny dots, then roll the trimmings into 12 tiny balls (about 5mm diameter). Dab one side of each dot with vodka and stick onto the inside of the pinwheels, repeating to create polka dots until all are used. Dab the centre of each pinwheel with vodka and press on one of the tiny balls to finish, flattening it gently. Leave the tray in a warm, dry place for about 24 hours or until the fondant is dry and hard.

7. To make the buttercream, beat the butter in a medium bowl until pale. Sift in the icing sugar and beat well until you have a smooth mixture. Blend in the vanilla extract. This can be made a day or two in advance and kept in the fridge, but bring to room temperature before using.

8. Once the pinwheels have hardened, assemble the cakes. Divide the buttercream evenly between the cake tops, shaping it into a small dome. Roll out the remaining red and blue fondant, again on parchment, to about 2mm thick. If you like, lay an embossing mat on top and roll over again to emboss the icing. Alternatively, use an embossed rolling pin directly on the icing. Stamp out six discs from each colour with the fluted cutter and lay one on top of each cake. Brush with lustre dust if you like. Place on a tray in the fridge for 20 minutes until firm.

9. Insert a pinwheel stick down through the centre of each cake. Arrange on a stand and serve at once.

Iced Fancies

Sipping tea and nattering with friends over a tiered stand full of pretty little cakes is what daydreams are made of! And you don't have to be a skilled cake decorator to tackle these, as they are fun and easy to create. Use paste food colouring rather than liquid as it doesn't affect the consistency of the icing. Keep the icing white if you prefer, or divide it into as many different colours as you wish.

MAKES 24

Juice of 1 lemon

25g caster sugar

280g shop-bought Madeira cake

450g icing sugar

6 tbsp boiling water

3 different paste food colourings

24 Crystallised Rose Petals (pages 186–7)

A KIT:

Large cooling rack set over a tray lined with parchment paper

24 mini paper muffin cases

1. First, make a lemon syrup. Pour the lemon juice into a small saucepan, add the sugar and slowly bring to the boil, stirring until dissolved. Remove from the heat and leave to cool for a few minutes.

2. Remove the crusts from the cake and then cut the cake into three across the width and then in half down the length. Lay each of the six chunks over on their sides and cut them into quarters to give 24 bite-sized pieces in total. Arrange spaced apart on the cooling rack and brush the lemon syrup all over their tops to soak in.

3. Sift the icing sugar into a large bowl and add the boiling water, stirring to give a smooth, pourable icing. Divide the icing evenly between three small bowls and add one food colouring to each bowl a tiny bit at a time until you get the shades you like.

4. Working quickly so the icing doesn't set, spoon each icing colour over one-third of the cake pieces to completely coat. The mixture should be thick enough to coat the cakes but not so thick that it doesn't run down the sides. Add a little more boiling water if necessary to give the right consistency. Sit a crystallised petal on top of each cake as you finish icing it. Leave for 2 hours so the icing hardens and the rose petals set firm.

5. Arrange 24 mini muffin cases on a large tray. Carefully remove the fancies from the cooling rack with a slice or palette knife and sit each one in a paper case. Arrange on a pretty cake stand to serve. These will keep for a day or two in an airtight container.

Raspberry & Chocolate Crepeathon Cake

This cake won't fail to impress, especially when guests see the stunning layers inside. Making all 24 crepes is indeed a bit of a 'crepeathon', but it can be done in stages (prepare half the batter at a time) and they can be made up to 2 days in advance and kept covered in the fridge, layered between parchment paper.

SERVES 16

CREPES:

500ml whole milk

250ml double cream

250g plain flour

50g cocoa powder

50g icing sugar

12 large eggs

1 tsp vanilla extract

Pinch of salt

75g unsalted butter

FILLING:

350g Raspberry Purée (page 185)

1.2kg full-fat cream cheese

50g icing sugar

TOPPING:

150ml double cream

375g fresh raspberries

175g Raspberry Purée (page 185)

100g Hazelnut Praline (page 183), optional

Fresh mint sprigs

ESSENTIAL KIT:

20cm non-stick crepe or frying pan

1. To prepare the crepe batter, place all the ingredients except the butter in a food processor and blend until smooth. This can be done by hand, with a whisk, but sift in the dry ingredients to avoid lumps. Pour into a large jug, cover with cling film and chill in the fridge for at least 30 minutes.

2. To cook, melt the butter in a small bowl in the microwave or a small pan on the hob. Using kitchen paper, rub a little melted butter all over the crepe pan and place on a medium heat. Add a small ladleful of batter (about 60ml) to the centre and swirl the pan. Cook for about 45 seconds until set on the bottom, flip, then cook for another 30 seconds until cooked through. Tip onto parchment paper and repeat to make 24 in total. Leave to cool.

3. Prepare the filling. If you haven't already, make the raspberry purée. Then beat the cream cheese in a large bowl to loosen. Add the purée, sift in the icing sugar and beat everything together well.

4. To assemble, lay one crepe in the centre of a cake stand and spread with about 4 tablespoons of the filling. Lay another crepe on top and spread with filling again. Continue to layer until all the crepes and filling are used up, finishing with a crepe. This can be made up to 24 hours in advance and kept covered in the fridge.

5. For the topping, softly whip the cream and spoon over evenly. Scatter the fresh raspberries on top, drizzle with a few tablespoons of the raspberry purée and pour the remainder into a small jug to serve. Crumble over the hazelnut praline, if using, scatter with mint sprigs and serve. Cut the cake in quarters and each quarter into four wedges to reveal the layers inside.

Giant Upside-Down Lollipop Cake

This is an eccentric take on a cake pop, in that it's made from cake crumbs blended with buttercream. The cakes can be made a few days ahead or frozen for even longer. If you have only two of the required tins, simply set two cakes at a time.

SERVES 12–16

Sunflower oil, for the tins

225g unsalted butter, softened

300g icing sugar

Finely grated zest of 2 lemons and juice of 1

3 × 280g shop-bought Madeira cakes

3 tbsp hundreds and thousands or other edible sprinkles

FILLING:

200g full-fat cream cheese

1 tbsp icing sugar

Seeds scraped from 1 vanilla pod

Juice of remaining 1 lemon

200g fresh strawberries, hulled and quartered

ESSENTIAL KIT:

4 × 10cm round, springform cake tins, at least 3cm high

Food processor

Paper straw

1. Oil the cake tins and line the sides with parchment paper.

2. Beat the butter in a large bowl until pale. Sift in the icing sugar and beat until smooth. Mix in the lemon zest and 3 tablespoons of juice.

3. In a food processor blitz the cakes to fine crumbs and tip into the mixture. Stir until thoroughly combined and divide evenly between the tins. Smooth with the back of a spoon, cover with cling film and chill in the fridge for 5–6 hours until firm. This can be prepared 2–3 days in advance.

4. Meanwhile, make the filling. Beat the cream cheese in a small bowl to loosen. Sift in the icing sugar and add the vanilla seeds. Pour in the juice of 1 lemon and beat well until smooth. This can be prepared up to a day in advance and kept covered in the fridge.

5. When ready to serve, scatter the sprinkles on a plate. Carefully remove each cake from its tin and peel off the paper. One by one, roll their sides firmly in the sprinkles until evenly covered. Sit one cake on a cake stand and spread with a quarter of the filling. Arrange a quarter of the strawberries on top. Repeat with another cake, more filling and strawberries until everything is used up. Press down gently as you pile the cakes up and finish with strawberries.

6. Your giant lollipop is taking shape and to finish it off insert a paper straw into the middle so it is sticking out the top. Ta-da! Serve at once but put in the fridge if there is any delay or the cake will start to soften and go mushy. It can be stored assembled like this for a few hours. The best way to cut this tower of loveliness is to remove the paper straw and then carefully lift the layers off, one at a time, onto a board. Cut each into 3–4 wedges and serve. Any uneaten cake can be stored covered in the fridge for a day or two.

Fruity Tea Brack

Here's a nifty alternative to your oven: a bread maker! It lets you create a warm, freshly baked cake with no fuss and without even having to be there to keep an eye on it. This fruity tea brack recipe is delicious warm, spread with a little butter and served with a cup of tea.

MAKES 8–10 slices

100g sultanas
100g raisins
150ml strong hot tea
1 tbsp brandy, optional
Sunflower oil, for greasing
50g unsalted butter
1 egg
1 tsp vanilla extract
175g self-raising flour
¼ tsp ground cinnamon
¼ tsp freshly grated nutmeg
150g soft light brown sugar
50g salted butter, softened, to serve

ESSENTIAL KIT:
Bread maker machine

1. Place the sultanas and raisins in a medium bowl, pour over the tea and brandy (if using) and leave to soak for at least 1 hour, or overnight if possible.

2. Set the bread maker machine up on a stable heatproof surface and plug it in. Grease the machine's loaf tin with a little oil on a piece of kitchen paper and set aside.

3. Melt the butter in a small saucepan on the hob or bowl in the microwave, remove from the heat and leave to cool.

4. Beat the egg in a small bowl and add to the loaf tin, along with the cooled butter, vanilla extract and dried fruits and their liquid. Do not stir. Sift in the flour, brown sugar, cinnamon and nutmeg, pressing the sugar through with a spoon if necessary. Again, do not be tempted to stir the mixture at any point.

5. Sit the loaf tin in position in the bread maker and close the lid. Then follow the machine manufacturer's guidelines for setting the machine to cook the cake. You will most likely just have to select the cake cooking setting and press start. The machine will first of all churn the cake mix, and you may need to scrape down the mixture from the sides with a rubber spatula occasionally until this ends. The cake will then probably take 1–1½ hours to cook, depending on your machine – it should beep when done. Leave the cake in the machine for a further 1–2 hours to finish cooking in the residual heat and to begin to cool down.

6. Remove and cut into 8 or 10 slices depending on its shape and size. This is most delicious served warm, spread with salted butter.

Jewelled Princess Castle Cake

Fit for a princess, this cake consists of a fudgy chocolate and biscuit base, decorated with lavish white chocolate shards. It is great for a large party as it cuts into nearly 100 pieces. If you only want one tier, halve all the quantities and set the cake in a 20cm tin. You can colour the shards if you like, as described on page 179. This is best assembled a day in advance to give it plenty of time to solidify in the fridge.

MAKES 48 wedges (or 96 fingers)

BISCUIT CAKE:

Sunflower oil, for the tins

800g milk chocolate

800g dark chocolate (at least 70% cocoa solids)

250g unsalted butter

5 × 400g cans condensed milk

1.2kg digestive biscuits

GANACHE:

400g white chocolate

200ml double cream

SHARDS:

50g whole almonds, roughly chopped

50g dried apricots, roughly chopped

50g dried cranberries, roughly chopped

50g golden sultanas, roughly chopped

900g white chocolate

1 tbsp edible gold balls

1 tbsp edible glitter

ESSENTIAL KIT OVERLEAF ➡

1. Oil the cake tins and line the sides with parchment paper.

2. Make the cake mix in two batches in case the quantities don't fit in one bowl. Snap both chocolates into a large bowl, add the butter and either melt in the microwave in 30-second blasts, stirring between each go, or over a pan of simmering water, shallow enough that the water doesn't touch the bowl. Once melted, stir in the condensed milk until well combined. Snap the biscuits in chunks into the mixture and stir until evenly coated.

3. Spoon into the smaller tin first, pressing down well and smoothing with the back of a spoon to prevent gaps and air pockets. Fill to the top and repeat with the second tin. Cover both with cling film and chill for at least 3 hours, or overnight, until set. The cakes can be made a week or two ahead and kept covered in the fridge.

4. Prepare the white chocolate ganache. Melt the chocolate in the same way as before. Warm the cream in a small saucepan over a gentle heat and remove just before it boils. Stir the cream into the melted chocolate until smooth and then leave to thicken and cool completely. Place covered in the fridge until ready to use.

5. To make the chocolate shards, line the baking sheets with parchment paper. Mix the chopped almonds and dried fruits in a small bowl. Melt the chocolate as before. Spoon 3 heaped tablespoons of melted chocolate onto one of the sheets and spread with the back of the spoon to about 20cm long, 10cm wide and

CONTINUED ➡

⇨ CONTINUED FROM OVERLEAF

1.2cm deep. Use the back of the spoon to drag the chocolate at one of the short ends into a point. Sprinkle evenly with a good pinch of the fruit and nut mixture, followed by a few edible balls and a light dusting of glitter, if using. Repeat to make three more shards of this size, spacing them apart on the tray. If the chocolate starts to thicken, simply warm it a little to loosen.

6. Then make a smaller size shard using 2½ heaped tablespoons of chocolate and spooning the rectangle to about 15cm long and 7.5cm wide, before creating the pointed end. Again, sprinkle all the bits on top and repeat to make about 20 smaller shards in total. Chill in the fridge for at least 1 hour until set hard. These can be prepared up to a month in advance and stored covered in the fridge.

7. When ready to assemble, beat the cool ganache to loosen it. Remove the cakes from the tins and peel off the paper. Spoon 2 tablespoons of ganache in the centre of a cake stand and stick on the larger cake. Spread another couple of tablespoons of ganache on this cake and stick the smaller cake well centred on top. Reserve 2 tablespoons of ganache and spread the remainder evenly all over the sides and tops of the whole cake with a palette knife.

8. Working quickly before the ganache sets, starting with the top tier, carefully stick the smaller chocolate shards up against each other, pointing upwards, all around the sides of both tiers. Spoon the reserved ganache into a pool on top of the cake. Stick the remaining four larger shards into this pool, just touching each other for support.

9. Voila, you have your stunning castle cake, best kept in the fridge until serving. To serve, carefully remove the shards to reveal the cakes, and place them on parchment paper. Lift off the top tier and cut each cake in half and then each half into 12 wedges. The wedges can then be cut into fingers if serving at a very large party. Lay on a platter, with the shards arranged on top. Leftovers will keep for a couple of weeks, well wrapped, in the fridge.

Upside-Down Banana 'Pan' Cakes

These cakes are cooked on a very low heat in individual blini pans. It is important to line the base of the pans with three layers of parchment paper to avoid burning the bottom of the cakes. They're best enjoyed freshly cooked, so if you only want a couple at a time keep the rest of the mix covered in the fridge for a day or two.

SERVES 4

50g unsalted butter, softened
+ extra for greasing

50g soft light brown sugar

1 large egg

50g self-raising flour

¼ tsp ground cinnamon

½ tsp vanilla extract

2 bananas

BUTTERSCOTCH SAUCE:

50g unsalted butter

100g soft light brown sugar

125ml double cream

1 tbsp whisky or dark rum, optional

TO SERVE:

75ml double cream

50g Caramelised Pecans or Walnuts (page 182), optional

ESSENTIAL KIT:

4 × 10cm blini pans

1. Line the base of each blini pan with three layers of parchment paper discs, but only the base to avoid a fire hazard. Then grease the top one and the sides of the pan with butter. Cut four 12.5cm squares of foil, grease one side of each, and set everything aside.

2. Beat the butter and sugar together in a medium bowl until pale and smooth. Beat in the egg and add the flour, cinnamon and vanilla extract, stirring together until smooth.

3. Peel the bananas and cut each into 20 slices. Arrange 10 slices in a single layer in the base of each pan. Divide the cake mix evenly on top, levelling it with the back of a spoon. Cover each pan tightly with the foil, buttered side down. Cook all four together over a very low heat for 6 minutes until just cooked through.

4. Meanwhile, make the sauce. Melt the butter in a small saucepan, add the sugar, cream and whisky or rum (if using) and stir until the sugar is dissolved and everything is well blended. Bring to the boil, then reduce to simmer for 6–8 minutes, stirring constantly, until thickened, before removing from the heat.

5. When each cake is cooked, remove from the heat and leave to stand for about 5 minutes. They will continue to cook, so don't be tempted to lift the covers. Meanwhile, softly whip the cream for serving.

6. When all the cakes are ready, remove the foil, place a small serving plate upside down on top of one pan and carefully flip both over to turn the cake out. Repeat with all cakes and drizzle with butterscotch sauce. Spoon on some whipped cream, crumble over the caramelised nuts, if using, and serve at once.

Rosewater & Lemon Krispie Roll

This quick and easy no-bake take on a Swiss roll can be assembled up to a day in advance. Use a mix of pink and white marshmallows for a different colour finish, or add food colouring to melted white marshmallows for any shade you fancy. You can roll the finished cake in finely chopped nuts or edible sprinkles if you like.

SERVES 12

Sunflower oil, for greasing

50g unsalted butter

300g pink marshmallows

1 tsp rosewater

150g Rice Krispies

FILLING:

400g full-fat cream cheese

4 tbsp icing sugar

Finely grated zest of 1 lemon

Seeds scraped from 1 vanilla pod

Small handful of Crystallised Rose Petals (pages 186–7), to decorate

ESSENTIAL KIT:

33cm × 23cm Swiss roll tin or baking tray, at least 2.5cm deep

1. Grease the tin with oil and line with parchment paper. Melt the butter in a large saucepan over a medium heat. Add the marshmallows and rosewater and stir until melted. Gently stir in the Rice Krispies until well coated.

2. Working quickly before it sets, spread the mixture into the tin, pressing down gently with the back of the spoon to smooth it out. If it is setting too quickly, lay a sheet of parchment paper on top and use the heel of your hand to spread it flat. Leave for about 30 minutes, covered with parchment, until cool and set.

3. For the filling, place the cream cheese in a medium bowl and sift in the icing sugar. Add the lemon zest and vanilla seeds, and beat until smooth. Cover with cling film and chill for at least 15 minutes.

4. When set, lift the cake out of the tin and peel the paper off the top and sides only. Spread the filling evenly just to the edges. Using a sharp knife, mark an indent along one short end, about 2cm in from the edge. From this end, use the parchment to help lift the cake and roll it over, peeling off the paper as you go. Roll it away from you, fairly tightly, until you reach the end. Sit it seam-side down on a serving platter. Scatter with crystallised rose petals and serve.

For an added twist . . .

★ **Chocolate and peanut butter roll:** Omit the rosewater and replace with 125g Nutella, adding it to white marshmallows. In the filling, omit the lemon zest and replace 100g of cream cheese with 100g smooth peanut butter. Roll the finished cake in 75g finely chopped hazelnuts or salted peanuts.

Cookie Monster Ice-Box Cake

This traditional American cake is made of cookies stacked with layers of creamy mascarpone. As it sits overnight, the cookies soften to a delicious cakey texture. Before you build the cake on a stand, make sure you have enough vertical space in your fridge, else use a serving plate instead. You can halve these quantities for a smaller cake, or assemble it in a dish for a cookie-mad take on tiramisu.

SERVES 24

250g mascarpone

Seeds scraped from 1 vanilla pod

1 litre double cream

600g dulce de leche caramel

96 double chocolate chip cookies, about 5cm wide (approx. 8–12 packets)

1 tsp cocoa powder, to dust

100g pecan or hazelnut Praline (page 183)

ESSENTIAL KIT:

Electric mixer or whisk (if you have one)

1. Place the mascarpone in a really large bowl, add the vanilla seeds and beat briefly to soften a little. Pour in the cream and whisk until soft peaks form. This is easiest with an electric mixer or whisk.

2. Reserve 75g of the dulce de leche caramel in a small bowl for later. Spread 1 tablespoon of the remainder onto a stand or serving plate in a 17cm circle. Then spread 12 cookies each with about a teaspoon of the caramel and arrange, caramel-side up, in a single layer on the stand: nine should fit in a circle with three in the middle. Spoon one-eighth (about 150g) of the mascarpone mixture on top and spread it in an even layer, almost to the edge of the cookies.

3. Spread 12 more cookies with caramel, arrange in the same manner on top of the cream, and spread with another eighth of the mascarpone. Repeat until you have 8 layers of cookies, finishing with a layer of the creamy mixture. Chill in the fridge for at least 8 hours or overnight. This can be prepared up to 24 hours in advance.

4. When ready to serve, gently warm the reserved caramel in a small pan or the microwave, just enough to loosen it. Leave to cool a little, then drizzle it back and forth across the top. Dust with cocoa powder. Break up the praline and scatter it over. To serve, cut the cake into 12 wedges. As the wedges are very tall, each can be halved horizontally. This will last another day in the fridge.

For an added twist . . .

★ Use peanut butter in place of dulce de leche. For drizzling, loosen with a splash of milk or cream.

Lemon Zuccotto with Passionfruit Syrup

Zuccotto is an Italian dessert that consists of a dome of cake filled with ice cream and resembling a 'little pumpkin' (which is what it translates as). This recipe is a twist on the Italian classic, filled with a lemon mousse instead of ice cream, and served covered in fragrant passionfruit syrup. You can use canned passionfruit pulp rather than fresh if you prefer. As the mousse filling is made with raw eggs, it is not advisable for very young children, pregnant women or anyone frail.

SERVES 8

CAKE SHELL:

2 × 280g shop-bought Madeira cakes (each roughly 15cm × 7.5cm)

Juice of 1 large lemon or 3 tbsp limoncello liqueur

FILLING:

6 gelatine leaves

Juice and finely grated zest of 3 lemons

4 eggs, separated

175g caster sugar

300ml double cream

SYRUP:

250ml passionfruit pulp (from about 12 fresh passionfruits)

100g caster sugar

ESSENTIAL KIT:

1.2-litre pudding basin

Electric whisk

1. Line the pudding basin with cling film, leaving a 10cm excess hanging over the edge.

2. For the filling, soak the gelatine leaves in a small bowl in just enough cold water to cover and leave for 5–10 minutes until softened.

3. Prepare the outer cake shell: if the Madeira cakes have crusts on the long sides (left and right), trim these off. Cut each cake lengthways into five slices about 1.5cm wide, then lay each slice flat and cut it diagonally in half so you get two long thin triangles.

4. Arrange about two-thirds of the triangles flat against the cling film in the basin, with the pointed ends at the bottom and the crust side of one slice against the cut edge of the next, until the bowl is lined. The slices may break up a little but simply press them back together in the basin. If the pointy ends start to pile up a bit in the bottom, just squidge them down with your fingers. Reserve the remaining cake slices for now. Brush the lemon juice all over the inside or use the limoncello if you prefer. Set aside while you prepare the filling.

5. Put the lemon juice and zest into a small saucepan and place on a low heat to warm through gently. Remove just as it comes to the boil. Squeeze the excess water from the now-softened gelatine, stir it into the lemon juice until dissolved and leave aside to cool.

CONTINUED ⇨

➔ CONTINUED FROM OVERLEAF

6. Place the egg yolks in a large bowl and add the sugar. Beat with an electric whisk until smooth and thickened slightly. Whisk the egg whites in another large bowl until soft peaks form – if you lift a bit of egg white on the whisk the peak should droop slightly. Whisk the cream in another bowl until just stiff.

7. Gently fold the cream into the egg yolk mixture, followed by the egg whites and then the lemon juice mixture, carefully folding until well blended. Spoon the filling into the cake-lined basin and smooth the top. Cover with the excess cling film and chill in the fridge for 2 hours until just set.

8. Meanwhile, make the passionfruit syrup. Scoop the passionfruit pulp into a small saucepan and add the sugar and 50ml of water. Bring to the boil over a medium heat, stirring until the sugar dissolves and then reduce the heat to simmer for 3–4 minutes until thick and syrupy. Set aside to cool and thicken further.

9. Once the filling has chilled for 2 hours, remove the zuccotto from the fridge. Open the cling film out and arrange the remaining cake slices over the top in an even layer (or two layers if you have that many) to cover. Place a saucer on top, pressing it down firmly, cover tightly with cling film and return to the fridge for a further hour or overnight until set. It can be made to this stage a day in advance.

10. When ready to serve, remove the saucer from the zuccotto, place a serving plate or cake stand upside down on top and turn the whole thing over. Remove the basin and carefully peel the cling film off. Gradually spoon about half of the passionfruit syrup over to drizzle down. Cut into eight wedges and serve with the remaining syrup in a small jug.

NO-BAKE
SLICES & BARS

Candied Popcorn Megabars

These megabars make fun additions to any party table or look great as gifts – why not create a mix of different colour schemes (as in the photo). Or you can make them in one colour if you like, in which case keep the mixture in one big batch rather than halving it. They are equally delicious au naturel in all their caramel glory if you choose not to use any food colouring at all. Go mad and add sprinkles, chopped nuts, dried fruits or even sweets to the mix before setting.

MAKES 8

2 tbsp sunflower oil + extra for greasing

150g corn kernels

100g condensed milk

100g glucose syrup

75g unsalted butter

50g soft light brown sugar

2 food colourings of your choice

ESSENTIAL KIT:

33cm × 23cm Swiss roll tin or baking tray, at least 2.5cm deep

String, if you like

1. Grease the tin with oil and line with parchment paper, leaving 5cm excess hanging over the edges to help with lifting out later.

2. Heat the oil in a really large saucepan over a low heat. Scatter the popcorn kernels in and swirl the pan to coat them evenly in oil. Cover with a tight-fitting lid and then leave for a few minutes to pop, without opening the lid. Once the popping subsides, remove from the heat, remove the lid and set aside.

3. Heat the condensed milk, glucose syrup, butter and sugar in a large saucepan over a medium heat, stirring occasionally, until the sugar dissolves and the mixture is bubbling. Remove from the heat and divide evenly between two large bowls. Add a different food colour to each one, adding a tiny dot at a time to give the intensity you like. Try blue and green together or red and yellow.

4. Tip half the popcorn into each bowl, discarding any unpopped kernels, and stir through evenly to coat. Then quickly stir both popcorns together, tip them out onto the prepared tray and spread evenly with the back of a spoon or the heel of your hand. Cover with a layer of parchment paper, followed by cling film and then chill in the fridge for about 3 hours until set.

5. Lift the popcorn slab out of the tin and peel off the paper. Cut along the length into quarters and then in half across the width to give eight bars in total. Wrap each one in parchment paper tied with string for a nice presentation if you like. These will keep for two days in an airtight container in the fridge.

Minty Chocolate Fudge Bars

The fudgy centre of these bars contrasts deliciously with the crisp base and smooth chocolate top. If mint isn't your thing, you can have a plain fudge layer by omitting the peppermint (or you can even make the fudge layer on its own as actual fudge!). These are also great as sweet canapés if cut into 36 tiny squares.

MAKES 12

BASE:

Sunflower oil, for greasing

50g milk chocolate

300g all-butter shortbread biscuits

25g cocoa powder

TOPPING:

200ml Milk Chocolate Ganache (page 183)

400g white chocolate

1 × 400g can condensed milk

½ tsp peppermint extract

ESSENTIAL KIT:

17.5cm square cake tin or baking dish

1. Grease the tin with oil and line with parchment paper, leaving 5cm excess hanging over the edges to help with lifting out later.

2. For the base, snap the chocolate into a small heatproof bowl and either melt in the microwave in 30-second blasts, stirring between each go, or over a pan of simmering water, shallow enough that the water doesn't touch the bowl. Once melted, remove from the heat, stir until smooth and leave to cool slightly.

3. Blend the biscuits in a food processor or seal in a food bag and bash with a rolling pin, until you have fine crumbs. Blitz or toss the cocoa powder through and stir the mix into the melted chocolate until well blended. Spread evenly in the tin. Chill in the fridge for 30 minutes to firm up.

4. Make the topping: prepare the chocolate ganache, if you haven't already done so, and leave to cool to body temperature.

5. Snap the white chocolate into a medium bowl and pour the condensed milk over. Either melt in the microwave in 30-second blasts, stirring between each go, or over a pan of simmering water, shallow enough that the water doesn't touch the bowl. Once melted and smooth, add the peppermint extract. Pour over the set base and spread evenly. Pour the ganache on top and also spread evenly. Leave to cool, then chill in the fridge for at least 2–3 hours until set.

6. Lift the slab out of the tin and peel off the paper. Using a long, sharp knife, dipped in boiling water and wiped dry between each cut, slice into 12 pieces. These will keep for 2–3 days, covered, in the fridge.

Oaty Jam Slices

Here's an interesting trio of tasty textures, with fruity jam sandwiched between a crisp biscuit base and a crumbly oaty top. The jam is quick and easy to make, and adds a lovely freshness, but you can use shop-bought if you're in a hurry. Jumbo oats are best as they are less dusty and crumbly than regular smaller flakes, but those also work fine in a pinch.

MAKES 9

BASE:

Sunflower oil, for greasing

50g unsalted butter

400g all-butter shortbread biscuits

JAM LAYER:

250g fresh raspberries

3 tbsp caster sugar

TOPPING:

150g rolled oats

50g whole blanched hazelnuts, roughly chopped

150ml maple syrup

ESSENTIAL KIT:

17.5cm square cake tin or baking dish

1. Grease the tin with oil and line with parchment paper, leaving 5cm excess hanging over the edges to help with lifting out later.

2. Melt the butter in a medium saucepan over a gentle heat or a bowl in the microwave. Blend the biscuits in a food processor, or seal in a food bag and bash with a rolling pin, to fine crumbs. Stir into the melted butter until well coated, then spread the mixture evenly into the tin. Chill in the fridge for 15 minutes to firm up.

3. To make the jam, place the raspberries and sugar in a small saucepan on a medium heat and simmer for about 10 minutes until the raspberries have softened and the jam is thick and syrupy. Leave to cool.

4. For the topping, divide the oats between two large dry frying pans and toast on a medium heat for about 5 minutes, tossing occasionally, until lightly golden. Tip the toasted oats into a bowl and use one of the pans to toast the chopped hazelnuts until golden also. Then toss with the oats.

5. Bring the maple syrup to a simmer in a large saucepan and let it bubble away for 2 minutes until thickened slightly. Tip the oats and hazelnuts into the syrup, stirring until evenly coated and set aside.

6. Spread the cooled jam evenly over the set base. Spoon over the oaty topping and press it down lightly with the back of a spoon. Cover with cling film and return to the fridge for 1–2 hours until set.

7. Lift the slab out of the tin, peel off the paper and cut into nine pieces. These will keep for 2–3 days covered in the fridge.

Heavenly Halva

This is a squidgy twist on traditional halva, made using dried fruits, which give it a delicious fudgy finish. You can decorate the tops with finely chopped nuts or a dusting of icing sugar instead of edible balls if you prefer, or just leave them plain. These use very few ingredients and are easy and speedy to make. They're also vegan and gluten free! Do you need any more convincing to give them a go?

MAKES 36

Sunflower oil, for greasing

200g pecan nuts

200g whole blanched almonds

50g sesame seeds

200g pitted Medjool dates

200g dried figs

5 tsp orange blossom water

50g edible gold balls, optional

ESSENTIAL KIT:

20cm square cake tin or baking dish

Food processor

1. Grease the tin with oil and line with parchment paper, leaving 5cm excess hanging over the edges to help with lifting out later.

2. Toss the pecan nuts, almonds and sesame seeds into a large dry frying pan and toast them over a medium heat, tossing regularly, until golden.

3. Tip the toasted nuts and seeds into a food processor and add the dates, figs and orange blossom water. Blend the mixture for a minute or two until completely smooth, scraping down the sides once or twice. Then spread the mixture out evenly in the prepared tin. Cover with cling film and chill for about 1 hour until firm.

4. Lift out of the tin and peel the paper down from the sides. Cut into six strips in each direction to give 36 small squares. Press some edible balls, if using, into the top of each one. Arrange the halva squares in neat rows on a serving platter and serve. These will keep for up to a week layered between parchment paper in an airtight container in the fridge.

Jammy Cornflake Marshmallow Chew Bars

Jammy by name and jammy by nature, as nobody will suspect how simple and quick these are to make! You don't have to use pink marshmallows, you can go for white or mixed colours instead. For an extra-indulgent finish, you can coat the final bars in melted chocolate: either half or fully immerse a bar at a time, allow the excess to drip off and leave to dry on a parchment-lined baking sheet.

MAKES 8

Sunflower oil, for greasing

300g pink marshmallows

50g unsalted butter

125g cornflakes

75g raspberry or strawberry jam

ESSENTIAL KIT:

17.5cm square cake tin or baking dish

1. Grease the tin with oil and line with parchment paper, leaving 5cm excess hanging over the edges to help with lifting out later. Sit a spoon in a jug of boiling water and set aside.

2. Place the marshmallows and butter in a large saucepan over a low heat and leave to melt, stirring occasionally with a lightly oiled spatula. Once melted and smooth, stir the cornflakes through until well coated.

3. Immediately tip the mixture into the prepared tin and, working really quickly before the mallow becomes stringy and sets, spread it out evenly with the hot spoon. Dollop the jam over the top and squidge it in a little with the hot spoon once again. Leave to cool and then cover with cling film and chill in the fridge for about 3 hours until set.

4. Once set, remove from the tin and cut into eight equal bars. These can be stored for up to a week layered between sheets of parchment paper in an airtight container in the fridge.

For an added twist . . .

★ Instead of the jam, add 25g of raisins and 25g of chopped pecans at the same time as the cornflakes.
★ Omit the jam, and add 2 pieces of stem ginger (from a jar), finely chopped, and 25g of chopped hazelnuts along with the cornflakes.

Fizz & Fireworks
Millionaire's Shortbread

You really will feel like a millionaire with these little nuggets of gold. The fizz and fireworks come from the popping candy in the base which will give your guests a nice surprise. Popping candy is available from good baking supply stores and online, and in fact from most good supermarkets now as well. But even without the popping candy these are still really special.

MAKES 12

BASE:
Sunflower oil, for greasing
50g unsalted butter
400g all-butter shortbread biscuits
2 tbsp popping candy

TOFFEE:
150g unsalted butter
150g soft dark brown sugar
1 × 400g can condensed milk

TOPPING:
100g dark chocolate (at least 70% cocoa solids)
100g milk chocolate

ESSENTIAL KIT:
17.5cm square cake tin or baking dish

1. Grease the tin with oil and line with parchment paper, leaving 5cm excess hanging over the edges to help with lifting out later.

2. Melt the butter for the base in a medium saucepan on the hob over a gentle heat or in a bowl in the microwave. Blend the biscuits in a food processor or seal in a food bag and bash with a rolling pin, until you have fine crumbs. Stir into the melted butter until well coated, then mix in the popping candy. Spread evenly into the tin. Chill in the fridge for 15 minutes to firm up.

3. For the toffee, heat the butter and sugar together in a medium saucepan over a gentle heat, stirring until the butter melts and the sugar dissolves. Add the condensed milk and bring gently to the boil, stirring constantly, to give a rich toffee sauce. Pour onto the set base, spreading evenly with the back of a spoon. Leave to cool completely and then cover with cling film and chill in the fridge for at least 1 hour until firm.

4. When it is almost set, prepare the topping. Snap both chocolates into a small heatproof bowl and either melt in the microwave in 30-second blasts, stirring between each go, or over a pan of simmering water, shallow enough that the water doesn't touch the bowl. Once melted, leave to cool to body temperature. Then, pour over the set toffee and spread evenly with the back of a spoon. Return to the fridge, covered, and leave for 1 hour until completely set.

5. Lift the set slab out of the tin and peel the paper from the sides. Cut into 12 pieces. These will keep for 2–3 days, layered between parchment paper, in an airtight container in the fridge.

Orange & Hazelnut 'Brownie' Bars

These are made from oats, dried fruits, nuts, peanut butter and of course chocolate. But despite having quite different ingredients to classic brownies, you will be pleasantly surprised at how brilliantly they work, with the roasted hazelnuts even adding a wonderful freshly baked smell and taste! Why would you ever need to turn on the oven?!

MAKES 16

Sunflower oil, for greasing

100g rolled oats

300g whole blanched hazelnuts, roughly chopped

100g dark chocolate (at least 70% cocoa solids)

Finely grated zest of 2 large oranges

200g cocoa powder

250g honey

4 tbsp smooth peanut butter

100g pitted prunes

100g dried apricots

1 tbsp icing sugar, to dust

ESSENTIAL KIT:

20cm square cake tin or baking dish

Food processor

1. Grease the tin with oil and line with parchment paper, leaving 5cm excess hanging over the edges to help with lifting out later.

2. Toast the oats in a large dry frying pan on a medium heat, tossing regularly for 5–6 minutes, until beginning to turn golden. Meanwhile, in a separate dry frying pan on a medium heat, toast the hazelnuts, tossing regularly, until golden.

3. Snap the chocolate into a large saucepan, add the orange zest, cocoa powder, honey and peanut butter. Allow to warm through over a low heat, stirring occasionally, until the chocolate has melted and the mixture comes together into a stiff dough. Remove from the heat.

4. Once toasted, tip the oats into a food processor and blitz to rough crumbs. Add the hazelnuts, prunes and apricots to the crumbs and blend to a smooth paste. Finally, add the chocolate dough and blend again until the mixture breaks up into fine crumbs.

5. Tip the mixture into the prepared tin, press it down and level it out evenly with your hands or the back of a spoon. Leave aside until cool and then cover with cling film and chill in the fridge for about 2 hours until firm.

6. Lift the brownie slab out of the tray and dust icing sugar through a fine sieve evenly over the top. Cut into four strips in both directions to give 16 squares in total and dive in. Any survivors will keep for 2–3 days in an airtight container in the fridge.

Trillionaire's Toffee Tiffin

As you bite into this triple-layered chocolate biscuit cake, gorgeous gooey toffee oozes out from between the crunchy base and the crisp chocolate top. You can omit the toffee layer if you fancy a speedier and less calorific bar, but let's face it: who wouldn't want to be a trillionaire?!

MAKES 12

BISCUIT BASE:

100g raisins

2 tbsp dark rum or orange juice

Sunflower oil, for greasing

300g rich tea biscuits

225g unsalted butter

4 tbsp clear honey

50g dark chocolate (at least 70% cocoa solids)

TOFFEE:

100g caster sugar

1 tbsp honey

150ml double cream

25g unsalted butter

TOPPING:

100g milk chocolate

50g dark chocolate (at least 70% cocoa solids)

ESSENTIAL KIT:

20cm square cake tin or baking dish

1. Leave the raisins to soak in the rum or orange juice in a small bowl for at least 1 hour or overnight, until you're ready to use.

2. Grease the tin with oil and line with parchment paper, leaving 5cm excess hanging over the edges to help with lifting out later. Seal the biscuits in a food bag and bash with a rolling pin into fairly rough pieces, then set aside.

3. Chop the butter into big chunks and place in a large saucepan with the honey. Snap in the chocolate and heat gently, stirring until smooth and melted together. Remove from the heat. Drain the raisins and add, followed by the biscuit pieces, and stir everything together until well coated. Tip into the prepared tin and spread evenly with the back of a spoon. Cover with cling film and chill in the fridge for about 30 minutes until set firm.

4. Meanwhile, make the toffee: place the sugar and honey in a small saucepan with 1 teaspoon of water over a low heat, and bring slowly up to a simmer, stirring until the sugar dissolves. Then simmer gently for 3–4 minutes, without stirring, until it turns golden brown in colour. Remove from the heat and slowly add the cream, being careful as it may splatter. It will look a bit of a mess but return to a gentle heat, stirring well and it will blend together in a minute or two. Finally, stir in the butter until melted and blended, then remove from the heat and leave to cool completely.

5. Once the tiffin base is set and the toffee is cool, spread the toffee evenly over the tiffin and return to the fridge for 30 minutes to firm.

6. Next, prepare the topping. Snap both chocolates into a medium heatproof bowl and either melt in the microwave in 30-second

blasts, stirring between each go, or over a pan of simmering water, shallow enough that the water doesn't touch the bowl. When melted, remove from the heat, stir gently to bring together and set aside until cool and the tiffin is ready. Then, pour it all over the toffee layer, spreading it out evenly with the back of a spoon – you can make a swirly pattern if you like. Return to the fridge for 30 minutes until set hard.

7. Lift the tiffin out of the tin and peel the paper from the sides. Using a long sharp knife, dipped in boiling water and wiped dry between each cut, slice into four equal-sized strips and then into thirds widthways to give 12 pieces. These will keep for up to a week layered between parchment paper in an airtight container in the fridge.

Rocky Road White Knuckle Ride

White chocolate gives an instant twist on a classic rocky road. The ingredients used here bring plenty of different colours, textures and flavours but if you aren't keen on Turkish delight, you can use fudge instead. In fact, fudge is delicious added into this mix, as are dried cranberries and apricots. The list is endless, so be as inventive as you like. Buckle up for a white knuckle ride!

MAKES 12

Sunflower oil, for greasing

25g desiccated coconut

500g white chocolate

150g marshmallows (large ones work better than mini)

150g Turkish delight

100g shelled green pistachios

100g mixed peel

ESSENTIAL KIT:

23cm square cake tin or baking dish

1. Grease the tin with oil and line with parchment paper, leaving 5cm excess hanging over the edges to help with lifting out later.

2. Toast the coconut in a wide, dry frying pan over a medium heat, tossing regularly, until golden. Remove from the heat and set aside.

3. Next, break the chocolate up into a large heatproof bowl. Either melt in the microwave in 30-second blasts, stirring between each go, or over a pan of simmering water, shallow enough that the water doesn't touch the bowl. When melted, remove from the heat and stir until smooth.

4. With scissors snip the marshmallows in half on top of the chocolate and then add the Turkish delight, pistachios, mixed peel and toasted coconut. Stir everything together well.

5. Pour into the tin and spread evenly with the back of a spoon. Move any large lumps around to fill any gaps or corners as necessary. Cover and refrigerate for at least 1 hour until set.

6. Lift out of the tin, cut into 12 pieces and stack in a pretty pile on a board to serve. These will keep for up to a week in an airtight container in the fridge (if they survive that long!).

Speckled Lemon Slices

These fabulously fudgy little fingers make an excellent partner to a cup of tea or coffee and are also a perfect sweet treat for vegans or coeliacs, as they are gluten free. They are just as delicious without the icing topping if you prefer them plain.

MAKES 18

350g unsalted cashew nuts

Sunflower oil, for greasing

Finely grated zest and juice of 3 lemons

150g raisins

150g dried apricots

3 tbsp poppy seeds

200g icing sugar

ESSENTIAL KIT:

20cm square cake tin or baking dish

Food processor

1. Place the cashew nuts in a medium bowl and cover by about 5cm with boiling water. Soak for about 15 minutes until slightly soft.

2. Meanwhile, grease the tin with oil and line with parchment paper, leaving 5cm excess hanging over the edges to help with lifting out later. Line a tray with parchment paper.

3. Place the lemon zest, the juice of 1 lemon, the raisins and apricots into a food processor. When the nuts are ready, drain well and add. Blend to give a smooth, thick paste, scraping down the sides if necessary. Add 2 tablespoons of the poppy seeds and blitz again to mix in. Spread the mixture evenly in the prepared tin, levelling with the back of a spoon. Sprinkle 2 teaspoons of the remaining poppy seeds evenly over the top and press gently to stick. Cover with cling film and chill for about 3 hours until firm.

4. Lift out of the tin and peel the paper away from the sides. Cut the slab into three strips and then halve widthways. Cut each of these six pieces into three fingers to give 18 in total. Arrange on the tray.

5. To finish, sift the icing sugar into a medium bowl, add 5 tablespoons of the remaining lemon juice, and mix to give a smooth and slightly runny icing glaze. Working quickly, stirring often to prevent it from forming a crust, spoon a heaped teaspoon of the glaze over each lemon slice, spreading with the back of the spoon and allowing it to run down the edges. If it seems too thick to do this, then add a tiny dash more lemon juice (or water) until you reach the right consistency. Sprinkle a pinch of the remaining poppy seeds over each one, before they set.

6. Arrange on a serving plate. These will keep for up to a week in an airtight container in the fridge.

White Chocolate, Macadamia & Cranberry Biscuit Bars

These chunky bars are super-easy to put together but will have everyone wondering how on earth you made them without baking. You can vary the recipe infinitely: go for milk or dark chocolate instead, use any type of biscuit and add extras like popping candy, chopped nuts, chocolate chips or crumbled Honeycomb (page 187). Have fun with a different combination every time.

MAKES 8 bars (or 16 smaller squares)

Sunflower oil, for greasing

400g white chocolate

1 × 400g can condensed milk

450g digestive biscuits

50g macadamia nuts, roughly chopped

50g dried cranberries

ESSENTIAL KIT:

23cm square cake tin or baking dish

1. Grease the tin with oil and line with parchment paper, leaving 5cm excess hanging over the edges to help with lifting out later.

2. Snap 300g of the chocolate into a large saucepan and add the condensed milk. Warm together over a low heat, stirring regularly until the chocolate has melted.

3. Meanwhile, blend the biscuits in a food processor, or seal in a food bag and bash with a rolling pin, to fine crumbs. Stir into the chocolate mix until well blended. Working fast before the mixture sets, spread into the tin with the back of a spoon. Set aside.

4. Toast the chopped macadamia nuts in a dry frying pan over a medium heat, tossing regularly, until golden. Tip into a small bowl and leave to cool.

5. Break the remaining 100g of chocolate into a small heatproof bowl. Either melt in the microwave in 30-second blasts, stirring between each go, or over a pan of simmering water, shallow enough that the water doesn't touch the bowl. Once melted, remove from the heat and stir until smooth. Pour over the biscuit base and spread evenly with the back of a spoon. Toss the cranberries in with the nuts and then scatter over the chocolate.

6. Cover with cling film and chill in the fridge for at least 1 hour or overnight, until firm. Remove from the tin and peel off the paper. Cut into eight rectangular bars. These can be halved again for 16 smaller squares if you prefer. They will keep for up to a week in the fridge, layered between parchment paper in an airtight container.

Chocolate, Date & Peanut Butter Bars

Medjool dates have a wonderful toffee squidginess, so be sure to seek out these rather than regular dates if you can. This recipe is as simple as blending the ingredients and spreading in a tin to set in the fridge, so there's no excuse not to give it a try. For extra naughtiness, dip the bars in melted dark, milk or white chocolate and leave to set.

MAKES 16

Sunflower oil, for greasing

350g pitted Medjool dates

100g dark chocolate (at least 70% cocoa solids), roughly chopped

75g rolled oats

3 tbsp crunchy peanut butter

Edible gold glitter dust, to decorate, optional

ESSENTIAL KIT:

17.5cm square cake tin or baking dish

Food processor

1. Grease the tin with oil and line with parchment paper, leaving 5cm excess hanging over the edges to help with lifting out later.

2. Blend the dates in a food processor to give a fairly smooth paste. Add the chocolate, oats and peanut butter. Blitz everything together until you have a chunky paste.

3. Spread the mixture out in the lined tin, levelling the surface with the back of a spoon. Cover with cling film and chill in the fridge for about 2 hours until set.

4. Lift out of the tin and peel the paper down from the sides. Brush the edible glitter dust (if using) all over the surface. Cut the slab into quarters and then each piece into four fingers. These will keep for up to a week in an airtight container in the fridge.

Gutsy Granola Bars

These granola bars are held together with peanut butter, puréed dates and maple syrup, and are surprisingly sturdy considering they are not baked. You can use almond or cashew nut butter in place of peanut butter if you prefer, and try honey or agave nectar instead of maple syrup. These are vegan-friendly (except if you use honey) and suitable for coeliacs if you choose gluten-free oats.

MAKES 10 bars (or 20 smaller squares)

Sunflower oil, for greasing

150g rolled oats

75g pecan nuts

50g pumpkin seeds

2 tbsp sesame seeds

50g raisins

2 tbsp golden linseeds

¼ tsp ground cinnamon

175g pitted Medjool dates

75g crunchy peanut butter

75g maple syrup

ESSENTIAL KIT:

17.5cm square cake tin or baking dish

Food processor

1. Grease the tin with oil and line with parchment paper, leaving 5cm excess hanging over the edges to help with lifting out later.

2. Toast the oats, pecan nuts, pumpkin and sesame seeds together in a large dry frying pan over a medium heat until golden brown, tossing regularly. Tip them into a large bowl and toss together with the raisins, linseeds and cinnamon.

3. Blend the dates in a food processor until smooth and tip into a medium saucepan. Add the peanut butter and maple syrup and cook over a medium heat for a few minutes, stirring, until well blended. Pour this mixture into the dry ingredients and stir everything well together until evenly coated.

4. Spoon the mixture into the prepared tin, spreading it out evenly with the back of a spoon. Cover with cling film and chill in the fridge for 1–2 hours until set firm.

5. Lift the granola slab out of the tin and peel the paper away from the sides. Cut into five even-sized strips, then cut these in half across to give 10 bars. Cut each one in half again to give 20 smaller squares if you prefer. These will keep for up to a week in an airtight container in the fridge.

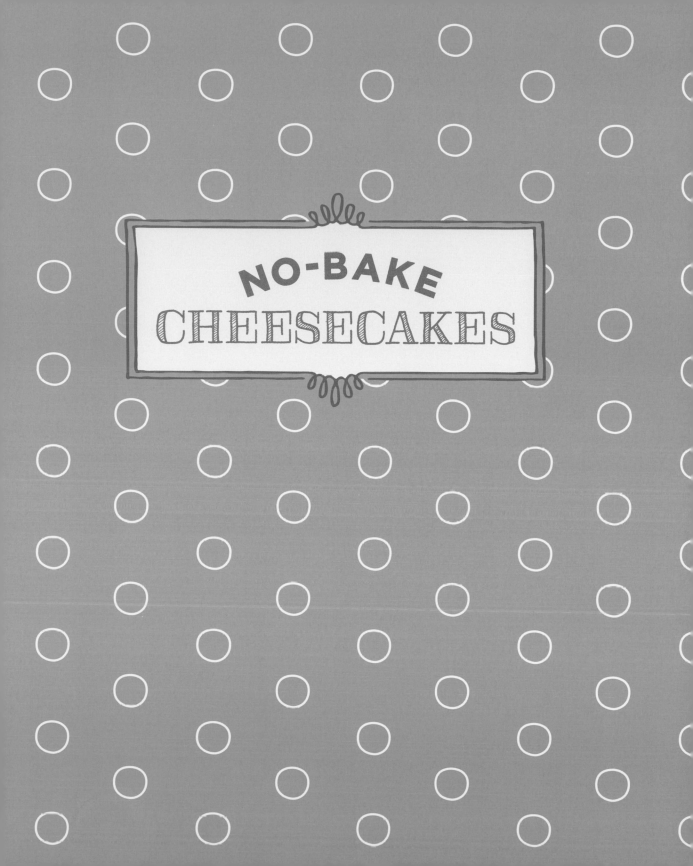

NO-BAKE
CHEESECAKES

Slightly Bonkers Pink Zebra Cheesecake with Marshmallow Pops

With its vivid colours, crazy pattern and poptastic topping, this cheesecake is bonkers on many levels. Beetroot juice is the secret to its colour – available from good supermarkets and speciality food stores, or make your own by whizzing a small beetroot in a juicer. Lollipop sticks can be bought from baking supply stores or online. This cheesecake is best made no more than half a day in advance, as the beetroot juice will eventually bleed into the white, spoiling the zebra effect.

SERVES 10

50g unsalted butter

200g pink wafer biscuits

5 tbsp beetroot juice (75ml)

6 gelatine leaves

800g full-fat cream cheese

200g sour cream

150g caster sugar

1 tsp vanilla extract

Finely grated zest and juice of 2 limes

MARSHMALLOW POPS:

2 tbsp edible sprinkles (of one type or mixed)

50g white chocolate

10 marshmallows

ESSENTIAL KIT:

20cm round, springform cake tin

10 × 10cm lollipop or cake pop sticks

Small piping bag, if you like

1. Melt the butter in a medium saucepan on the hob or in a bowl in the microwave. Blend the biscuits in a food processor, or seal in a food bag and bash with a rolling pin, until you have fine crumbs. Stir the crumbs and 1 tablespoon of the beetroot juice into the melted butter to coat evenly and then spread in the cake tin. Chill in the fridge for 15 minutes to firm up.

2. Divide the gelatine leaves into two stacks of three, place each stack in a small bowl, pour over just enough cold water to cover and soak for 5–10 minutes until softened.

3. Beat the cream cheese in a large bowl or food mixer until smooth and loosened up a little. Beat in the sour cream, sugar and vanilla extract until well blended. Divide the mixture in half evenly between two medium bowls (about 575g each). Add the lime zest to one half of mixture and set aside for a minute.

4. In a pan on the hob or bowl in the microwave, warm the lime juice. Do the same with the remaining 4 tablespoons of beetroot juice in a separate pan or bowl. Remove both from the heat. Squeeze the excess water from the now-softened gelatine and drop one batch into the lime juice and the other into the beetroot juice, stirring both until dissolved. Leave to cool for a few minutes. Then, pour the cool lime juice into the creamy mixture with the lime zest, folding it in until well combined. Pour the cool beetroot juice into the other creamy mixture, again folding it in well.

CONTINUED

CONTINUED FROM OVERLEAF

5. Now for the fun bit. Using a different tablespoon for each mixture and starting with the pink one, drop a spoonful of it into the centre of the biscuit base. Then drop a spoonful of the white mixture into the centre of the pink blob, followed by a pink spoonful into the centre of the white blob. Continue adding spoonfuls into the centre. The mixtures will push out towards the edge of the tin and then grow up the sides. Give them a little help to spread every so often, by gently banging the tin on your worktop. You will see an exciting swirly marbled pattern emerging. Continue until both mixtures are used up. Cover with cling film and chill in the fridge for at least 3 hours or overnight, until set firm.

6. Make the marshmallow pops. Pour the sprinkles into small bowls (or one bowl if using all the same type). Snap the chocolate into a small heatproof bowl and either melt in the microwave in 30-second blasts, stirring between each go, or over a pan of simmering water, shallow enough that the water doesn't touch the bowl. When melted, remove from the heat and stir until smooth.

7. Stick a lollipop stick into the base of a marshmallow to create a pop and repeat for all ten. Either dip the top of the marshmallow into the chocolate to half-coat or use a small piping bag to pipe melted chocolate around it in a helter-skelter pattern. Then dip the pops in the sprinkles as you wish. Pierce the finished pop sticks into an egg box or insert in the holes of a wire rack so they stand upright and leave to set. These can be made a day in advance and stored in an airtight container between sheets of parchment, once set.

8. When ready to serve, run a knife around the edge of the cheesecake to loosen from the tin, then carefully remove and slide onto a cake stand or serving plate. Stick the marshmallow pops all over the top of the cheesecake for a slightly bonkers effect and serve. Cut into ten wedges each with a pop on top.

Mango & Passionfruit Muffin-Cup Cheesecakes

Muffin cases make unusual moulds for these delicious cheesecakes. Tropical mango and passionfruit contrast electrically with the creamy filling and crunchy gingernut base – once you taste these you're guaranteed to be back for more!

MAKES 12

4 gelatine leaves

75g unsalted butter

175g gingernut biscuits

Finely grated zest and juice of 1 lime

400g full-fat cream cheese

100g caster sugar

Seeds scraped from 1 vanilla pod

250ml double cream

150g Mango Purée (page 185)

3 passionfruit

ESSENTIAL KIT:

12-hole muffin tin

12 paper muffin cases

1. Soak 3 gelatine leaves in just enough cold water to cover, for 5–10 minutes until soft. Meanwhile, line the tin with muffin cases.

2. Melt the butter in a medium saucepan on the hob or in a bowl in the microwave. Blend the biscuits in a food processor, or seal in a food bag and bash with a rolling pin, to fine crumbs. Stir into the melted butter to coat evenly and divide equally between the cases, about 2 tablespoons in each. Use the base of a small glass to press the mixture into the cases. Chill for 10–15 minutes to firm up.

3. Setting aside the lime zest, warm the lime juice in a small pan on the hob or in a bowl in the microwave until just boiling. Squeezing off the excess water, stir the now-softened gelatine into the juice until dissolved. Leave to cool completely.

4. Beat the cream cheese in a large bowl or food mixer to loosen. Add the lime zest, sugar and vanilla seeds, and beat for 1–2 minutes until smooth. Add the cream and beat for another minute until thickened, then stir in the lime juice mixture. Divide evenly between the paper cases, smoothing the tops with the back of a spoon. Chill for 15 minutes until just set.

5. Meanwhile, soak the remaining gelatine leaf as before. Prepare the mango purée, if you haven't already, and warm it in a small pan on the hob or in a bowl in the microwave, until just boiling. Remove from the heat. Squeezing off the excess water, stir the softened gelatine into the purée until dissolved. Leave to cool completely.

6. Once cool, divide the purée evenly over the cheesecakes. Chill for at least 1 hour, until set firm. When ready to serve, carefully peel off the cases and arrange on plates. Scoop the passionfruit seeds and juice over each cheesecake. Serve immediately.

Coconut & Almond Pashka with Poached Nectarines

Pashka is a Russian dish traditionally eaten at Easter, made with ingredients forbidden during Lent. It usually consists of a sweet cheese and custard mixture containing candied fruits and nuts, set in a domed mould. This version is rather like a baseless cheesecake and is served with nectarines and waffle biscuits.

SERVES 6–8

6 gelatine leaves

1 × 400ml can coconut milk

5 egg yolks

4 tbsp clear honey

Seeds from 1 vanilla pod

Finely grated zest and juice of 2 limes

50g flaked almonds

300g full-fat cottage cheese

300g full-fat cream cheese

250g sour cream

100g unsalted butter, softened

Small handful of Crystallised Rose Petals (pages 186–7)

6–8 waffle biscuits, to serve

NECTARINES:

200g caster sugar

1 vanilla pod and its scraped seeds

4 nectarines, quartered and stoned

ESSENTIAL KIT:

Food processor

1.7-litre brioche mould, jelly mould or bowl

1. Soak the gelatine in just enough cold water to cover, for 5–10 minutes until soft.

2. Gently heat the coconut milk in a medium pan until just boiling. Beat the egg yolks, honey, vanilla seeds and lime zest in a large bowl until combined. Gradually pour the coconut milk into the egg mix, stirring continuously. Pour the whole mixture back into the pan and cook gently for 2–3 minutes, stirring until thickened, then remove. Squeezing off the excess water, stir the softened gelatine into the custard until dissolved. Pour into a wide dish to cool quickly, placing cling film directly on the surface to prevent a skin forming.

3. Toast the almonds in a wide dry frying pan, tossing regularly, until golden. Blitz the lime juice, cottage cheese, cream cheese, sour cream and butter in a food processor until smooth. Pour into a large bowl and fold in the cooled custard and almonds until well mixed. Pour into the mould, cover and chill for at least 4 hours, until set.

4. In a wide saucepan, slowly bring 200ml of water to the boil with the sugar, stirring until dissolved. Boil for 2 minutes. Add the vanilla pod and seeds, and the nectarines. Reduce the heat and poach very gently for 8–10 minutes until soft. Using a slotted spoon, scoop the nectarines into a bowl. Return the syrup to the boil for 4–5 minutes, until reduced. Pour over the nectarines and leave to cool. Cover with cling film and chill until serving.

5. To serve, dip the mould in boiling water for 10–20 seconds. Hold a plate upside down on top, turn over, shake gently and the pashka will drop out. Spoon some nectarines and syrup on top, decorate with rose petals and serve with the remaining fruit and waffle biscuits.

Chocolate & Banana Polka-Dot Cheesecake

This unconventional cheesecake loaf reveals exciting polka dots inside when cut! There are a few stages to the recipe, so allow plenty of time and take care when piping the dots. If you find them tricky, you can instead create a marbled effect by simply swirling the chocolate mix with the plain one.

SERVES 12

155g pack Maltesers

6 gelatine leaves

3 ripe bananas (giving about 300g when peeled)

Juice of 1 lemon

500g mascarpone

250g full-fat cream cheese

100ml maple syrup

2 tbsp boiling water

100g dark chocolate (at least 70% cocoa solids)

50g unsalted butter

150g double chocolate chip cookies

1 tsp ground cinnamon

ESSENTIAL KIT:

900g loaf tin, about 23cm × 9cm, and 7.5cm deep

Food processor

Piping bag fitted with a 1.5cm plain nozzle or a disposable piping bag snipped to this size opening

1. Line the tin with cling film, leaving about 10cm excess hanging over each edge. Arrange the Maltesers neatly in a single layer in the base of the tin. There may be some leftovers – chef's treat!

2. Soak the gelatine leaves in a small bowl in just enough cold water to cover and leave for 5–10 minutes until softened.

3. Break the bananas into a food mixer, add the lemon juice and beat for a minute until well mashed. Add the mascarpone, cream cheese and maple syrup and beat for a minute or two until smooth and well mixed. Leave aside until needed.

4. Measure the boiling water into a small bowl. Squeeze the excess water from the now-softened gelatine and stir the gelatine into the boiled water until dissolved. Leave to cool.

5. Snap half of the chocolate into a small heatproof bowl and either melt in the microwave in 30-second blasts, stirring between each go, or over a pan of simmering water, shallow enough that the water doesn't touch the bowl. Remove from the heat and leave to cool to body temperature.

6. Melt the butter in a medium saucepan on the hob or in a bowl in the microwave. Blend the cookies in a food processor, or seal in a food bag and bash with a rolling pin, until you have fine crumbs. Tip into the melted butter, add the cinnamon and stir well to coat evenly. Set aside.

7. Returning to the now-cool gelatine mixture, gently fold it into the creamy filling until well combined. Reserve 300g of the mixture in a

CONTINUED ➡

⇨ CONTINUED FROM OVERLEAF

separate bowl. Dollop half of the remaining mixture into the tin and gently spread it out, being careful not to disturb the Maltesers.

8. Now for the fun polka-dot bit. Fold the now-cooled chocolate into the reserved mixture until well blended. Spoon this into the piping bag. Insert the tip of the nozzle or bag into the filling close to one corner of the tin until you just touch the Maltesers. Squeeze the bag gently to form one polka dot and then pull the bag up and out to release. Repeat twice more in a row across the width to give three polka dots. Move along by 2 or 3cm and repeat another row, continuing to do this all along the length, using up half the chocolate mixture.

9. Then add the remaining white filling mixture and spread the top level. Repeat the rows of dots with the remaining chocolate mixture, inserting the nozzle or bag to the same depth as before (as you won't have the Maltesers as a guide this time).

10. Finally, tip the cookie base evenly over the top, pressing it down with the back of a spoon. Cover with the excess cling film, chill in the fridge for about 5 hours until set. If you plan on leaving it in the fridge any longer than this, it is advisable to turn the cheesecake out onto its serving plate when set or the Maltesers may become a bit soggy.

11. To turn out, open the cling film, place an upturned rectangular serving plate on top and turn the whole thing over. Lift the tin off and carefully peel away the cling film to reveal the Maltesers. When ready to serve, melt the reserved chocolate in the same way as before and, once slightly cooled, drizzle it back and forth over the top of the cheesecake, so it runs down the sides a little. Cut into 12 even-sized slices to reveal the polka dots and serve.

No-Wait Mini Lemon & Ginger Cheesecakes

These instant puds are perfect for when you have limited time but want to whip up something impressive. The base is made with almonds and dates, which is a refreshing change from the usual biscuit-crumb mixture. You can dream up all kinds of different flavour ideas for the cheesecake part, such as crushed raspberries or chocolate chips. They also look great presented in mini kilner jars, teacups or small bowls.

SERVES 4

75g whole almonds

500g mascarpone

50g icing sugar

Finely grated zest and juice of 2 lemons

Seeds scraped from 1 vanilla pod

3 pieces of stem ginger (from a jar), finely chopped + a little of the syrup, to serve

25g pitted Medjool dates

4 fresh mint sprigs, to serve

ESSENTIAL KIT:

Food processor

4 × 175ml glasses

1. Place the almonds in a small bowl and pour boiling water over to cover by about 2.5cm. Soak for 5–10 minutes.

2. Place the mascarpone in a large bowl and sift in the icing sugar. Add the lemon zest and juice, the vanilla seeds and two-thirds of the chopped stem ginger (reserving the rest for serving). Stir everything together well and set aside.

3. Drain the almonds, pop them in a food processor with the dates and blitz until roughly chopped. Leave to cool a little and then spoon the mixture evenly between the serving glasses, pressing it down gently into the bottom. Spoon the mascarpone mixture on top, dividing evenly between the glasses. These can be prepared up to 24 hours in advance.

4. When ready to serve, spoon the reserved chopped ginger in a little pile in the centre of each glass, before drizzling with a little of the ginger syrup. Decorate with a mint sprig and serve.

Upside-Down & Inside-Out Peanut Butter Cheesecake Bombe

If the mere mention of peanut butter and cheesecake in the same sentence has you aquiver, then this is the recipe for you. Under the luscious chocolate ganache is a crisp cookie shell; cutting it open reveals a moreish peanut butter cheesecake centre. You can also make mini versions in dariole moulds or mini pudding basins.

SERVES 8

Sunflower oil, for greasing

3 gelatine leaves

100g unsalted butter

2 × 154g packs Chocolate Creme Oreo cookies

2 tbsp boiling water

400g full-fat cream cheese

225g smooth peanut butter

200ml double cream

75g golden caster sugar

200ml Chocolate Ganache (page 183)

25g salted peanuts, roughly chopped

ESSENTIAL KIT:

1.2-litre bowl (roughly 16cm across the top and 10cm deep)

Food processor

1. Grease the inside of the bowl with oil and line with a double layer of cling film, leaving 10cm excess hanging down the sides.

2. Soak the gelatine leaves in a small bowl, in just enough cold water to cover, for 5–10 minutes until softened.

3. Melt the butter in a medium saucepan on the hob or in a bowl in the microwave. Blend the biscuits in a food processor, or seal in a food bag and bash with a rolling pin, until you have fine crumbs. Stir into the melted butter to coat evenly and tip into the prepared bowl. Press the mixture over the entire inside of the bowl in an even layer. Chill in the fridge for 15 minutes to firm up.

4. Measure the boiling water into a small bowl. Squeeze the excess water from the now-softened gelatine and stir the gelatine into the boiled water until dissolved. Leave to cool.

5. Blitz the cream cheese, peanut butter, cream and sugar in a food processor until well blended, scraping the sides as necessary. When the gelatine mixture is cool, add to the food processor and blitz again for a few seconds. Spoon into the biscuit bowl, levelling the top with the back of a spoon. Cover with the excess cling film and chill in the fridge for at least 6 hours or overnight, to set.

6. When ready to serve, prepare the chocolate ganache if you haven't yet; else gently warm through. Open the cling film on the cheesecake and pull up a little to loosen from the bowl. Place an upturned plate or cake stand on top and turn the whole thing over. Lift the bowl off and carefully peel away the cling film. Spoon ganache over the dome, scatter with chopped peanuts and serve.

Candy-Stripe Blueberry Cheesecake

There may seem a lot of stages here, but it's simply a matter of splitting the mixture to create three different-coloured layers. If you're not in a stripy mood, just make the whole thing in one shade, keeping the gelatine, blueberry purée and creamy mixture in single batches. But if you do make the extra effort with the layers, you will be rewarded with a stunning candy-stripe finish that will wow your friends. Vary this recipe with any other berry purée you fancy.

SERVES 12

10 gelatine leaves

75g unsalted butter

200g digestive biscuits

1 tsp ground cinnamon

375g Blueberry Purée (page 185)

600g full-fat cream cheese

175g caster sugar

200g crème fraîche

800ml double cream

125g fresh blueberries

Small handful of fresh mint sprigs

ESSENTIAL KIT:

17.5cm round, loose-bottomed cake tin, 10cm deep

Food mixer

1. Line the sides of your cake tin with parchment paper (do not grease). If the tin isn't quite the required 10cm deep, just use a strip of paper that is at least that tall and so stands higher than the top of the tin. This will work to hold the top of the cheesecake in place.

2. To make the filling, the gelatine leaves will need to be soaked in three separate batches, one for each layer, so they don't stick together. Place 3 leaves in one large bowl, 3 in another and finally 4 leaves in a third bowl that is distinguished in some way so you don't mix them up. Pour just enough cold water over each batch to cover and leave to soak for 5–10 minutes until softened.

3. To make the base, melt the butter in a medium saucepan on the hob or in a bowl in the microwave. Blend the biscuits in a food processor, or seal in a food bag and bash with a rolling pin, until you have fine crumbs. Tip into the melted butter, add the cinnamon and stir well to coat evenly. Spread evenly in the prepared tin. Chill in the fridge for 15 minutes to firm up.

4. If you haven't already, make the blueberry purée, then gently heat it in a small saucepan on the hob or in a bowl in the microwave until it just comes to the boil and remove from the heat. Drain the water off the now-softened gelatine, squeeze the excess water from each bundle and pop them back in their respective bowls. Pour 50g of blueberry purée into one of the bowls with three gelatine leaves, 100g into the other bowl with three leaves, and then the remaining

CONTINUED ➡

CONTINUED FROM OVERLEAF

225g of purée into the bowl with four leaves. Stir each one until the gelatine dissolves and leave to cool.

5. Beat the cream cheese and sugar together in a food mixer until well combined and smooth. Quickly beat in the crème fraîche and add 650ml of the cream. Beat the mixture for a couple of minutes until softly whipped up, taking care not to allow it to become too stiff. Cover with cling film and set aside in the fridge.

6. Once the bowls of gelatine and purée are cool, divide the creamy mixture equally (in roughly 525g batches) between the three bowls and gently fold it in until well combined. Spoon the lightest coloured mixture onto the biscuit base, spreading it out evenly. Add the middle shade in the same way, then cover with cling film and chill in the fridge for 30 minutes until firm. Finally, add the darkest layer, smooth the top out evenly, cover with cling film and chill in the fridge for at least 5 hours or overnight until completely set.

7. Carefully remove from the tin and onto a cake stand or serving plate. Gently peel the paper away to reveal the stripes. Lightly whip the remaining 150ml of cream to soft peaks and spoon it on top. Scatter with the fresh blueberries, decorate with mint sprigs and serve.

Death by Chocolate & Blackberry Cheesecake

Three luscious layers of chocolate will have you creeping to the fridge in the middle of the night for more of this sinful creation. The Oreo cookie base, creamy chocolate cheesecake and rich ganache topping are finished with tart blackberries, which are to the chocolate like red wine is to cheese!

SERVES 12

Sunflower oil, for greasing

125g unsalted butter

2 × 154g packs Chocolate Creme Oreo cookies

300g dark chocolate (at least 70% cocoa solids)

600g full-fat cream cheese

1 × 400g can condensed milk

200ml Chocolate Ganache (page 183)

200g crème fraîche, to serve

BLACKBERRY SAUCE:

375g fresh blackberries

Juice of ½ orange

25g icing sugar

2 tbsp crème de cassis (or blackcurrant cordial)

ESSENTIAL KIT:

20cm round, springform cake tin

Food processor

1. Grease the tin with oil and line the base and sides with parchment.

2. Melt the butter in a medium saucepan on the hob or in a bowl in the microwave. Blend the biscuits in a food processor, or seal in a food bag and bash with a rolling pin, to fine crumbs. Stir into the melted butter to coat evenly and press onto the tin base and about 4cm up the sides. Chill for 15 minutes to firm up.

3. Snap the chocolate into a small heatproof bowl and either melt in the microwave in 30-second blasts, stirring between each go, or over a pan of simmering water, shallow enough that the water doesn't touch the bowl. Once melted, leave to cool to body temperature.

4. Briefly beat the cream cheese in a large bowl. Beat in the condensed milk and cooled chocolate until smooth. Spread evenly on the base. Cover with cling film and chill for at least 4 hours, until firm.

5. Reserve two-thirds of the blackberries (ideally the smallest ones) in a bowl. Pop the rest in a food processor, add the orange juice, icing sugar and crème de cassis (or cordial) and blitz until smooth. Pass through a fine sieve over the reserved berries. Cover and chill.

6. If you haven't already, make the chocolate ganache and leave to cool. Otherwise, just gently re-warm to loosen and leave to cool. It should be spreadable but cool enough not to melt the cheesecake. About an hour before the cheesecake is ready, spread the ganache evenly over the top and return to the fridge to set.

7. To serve, carefully remove the cheesecake from the tin and peel off the paper. Sit on a cake stand, and spoon the reserved blackberries and berry sauce on top. Serve with crème fraîche.

Mini Chestnut Cheesecake Sundaes

Chestnut purée may seem an unusual cheesecake ingredient but its distinctive flavour and smooth texture work beautifully with crunchy cookie crumbs. Assemble just before serving so the cookies don't get soggy. Maraschino cherries look best with stems still attached if you can find them – try delis, speciality food stores or even cocktail bars. Most supermarkets sell them without stems.

SERVES 6

25g whole blanched hazelnuts, finely chopped

100g double chocolate chip cookies

175g unsweetened chestnut purée (or sweetened if it's all you can find)

250g mascarpone

25g caster sugar

TO DECORATE:

2 tbsp edible sprinkles of your choice

50g white chocolate

75ml double cream

1 tbsp edible pearls

6 maraschino cherries with stems

6 homemade flags

ESSENTIAL KIT:

6 × 125ml glasses

Food processor (if using unsweetened chestnut purée)

1. First, decorate the glasses. Pour the sprinkles into a small bowl. Snap the chocolate into a small heatproof bowl and either melt in the microwave in 30-second blasts, stirring between each go, or over a pan of simmering water, shallow enough that the water doesn't touch the bowl. When melted, brush chocolate around the top of each glass in a 1cm-thick band on the inside and outside. Dip each glass into the sprinkles and leave to set.

2. Toast the hazelnuts in a dry frying pan over a medium heat, tossing regularly, until golden. Blitz the cookies in a food processor, or seal in a food bag and bash with a rolling pin, until you have rough crumbs. Stir the hazelnuts into the cookie crumbs and set aside.

3. If using unsweetened chestnut purée, blend in a food processor to get rid of any graininess. Beat the mascarpone and sugar in a medium bowl until smooth. Fold the chestnut purée into the mascarpone until well mixed. (If using sweetened chestnut purée simply beat with the mascarpone and omit the sugar.)

4. To assemble, spoon a tablespoon of crumb mixture into each glass. Top with 2 tablespoons of the creamy mixture, being careful not to mess up the sides or top. Add second layers of biscuit and creamy filling and finish with biscuit. You can serve straight away, or for a firmer finish, cover with cling film and chill for 1 hour.

5. When ready to serve, softly whip the cream in a medium bowl. Dollop a spoonful onto each sundae, sprinkle with edible pearls and sit a cherry proudly on top, stalk upright. For ultimate cute factor, decorate with homemade flags. Serve immediately.

Raspberry & White Chocolate Cheesecake Pops

These white-chocolate-coated wedges of cheesecake can be eaten frozen or defrosted. You can buy wooden ice lolly sticks from good baking supply stores or online. Sprinkle the molten chocolate with anything you like: try crumbled Honeycomb (page 187), chopped dried fruit, sprinkles or edible glitter.

MAKES 18 (+ 4 smaller offcuts)

Sunflower oil, for the tin

6 gelatine leaves

75g unsalted butter

200g digestive biscuits

300g fresh raspberries

100g caster sugar

Finely grated zest and juice of 1 lime

400ml double cream

300g full-fat cream cheese

250g mascarpone

25g whole blanched almonds, finely chopped

600g white chocolate

ESSENTIAL KIT:

18cm × 25cm baking tin, at least 4cm deep

Food processor

22 wooden ice lolly sticks

1. Oil the baking tin and line with parchment paper, leaving 5cm excess hanging over the sides to help with lifting out later.

2. Soak the gelatine leaves in a small bowl, in just enough cold water to cover, for 5–10 minutes until softened.

3. Melt the butter in a medium saucepan on the hob or in a bowl in the microwave. Blend the biscuits in a food processor, or seal in a food bag and bash with a rolling pin, until you have fine crumbs. Stir into the melted butter until well coated and spread evenly in the tin. Chill in the fridge for 15 minutes to firm up.

4. Tip the raspberries, sugar, lime zest and juice into a food processor and blitz to a smooth purée. Heat 100ml of this in a small saucepan on the hob or in a bowl in the microwave. Squeezing off the excess water, stir the now-softened gelatine into the warm purée until dissolved. Mix this back into the original purée and leave to cool.

5. Beat the cream, cream cheese and mascarpone together in a large bowl or food mixer until smooth. Pour in the purée and beat again for a moment until well blended. Pour onto the biscuit base and spread evenly with the back of a spoon. Cover with cling film and chill in the fridge for at least 3 hours, to set.

6. When ready, take two large trays that will fit in the freezer and line with parchment paper. Lift the cheesecake out of the tin onto a board, peel the paper down from the sides and cut in half

CONTINUED ⇨

➡ CONTINUED FROM OVERLEAF

lengthways. Using the tip of a knife, score a little mark every 5cm on one long side of one half. Then do the same along the centre cut line, but with the first notch 2.5cm in from the end and then at 5cm intervals again. Now, it's a case of joining up the dots. Starting from one corner on the original side and always working diagonally, cut across to the first mark on the centre line and back to the first mark on the original side. You should have a small end piece and a triangle. Continue in this way to the end, to give nine triangles and two end pieces. Repeat with the other half. Arrange spaced apart on the prepared trays as you go.

7. Insert a wooden lolly stick into the side at the bottom of each triangle, pushing it in about 5cm. Cover the trays with cling film and freeze for at least 4 hours or overnight, until really firm.

8. When the pops are set (leave in the freezer for now), toast the almonds in a dry frying pan, tossing regularly, until golden. Remove from the heat and leave to cool. Snap the chocolate into a small heatproof bowl and either melt in the microwave in 30-second blasts, stirring between each go, or over a pan of simmering water, shallow enough that the water doesn't touch the bowl. When melted, remove from the heat and stir until smooth.

9. Remove the pops from the freezer and hold one by the stick upside down over the melted chocolate. Spoon a large spoonful over the pop, allowing it to run down all sides, using the back of the spoon to spread if necessary. The chocolate will set quickly so work fast. Allow the excess to drip off and then return the pop to the tray, sprinkling with chopped nuts. Repeat with all the pops. Freeze for at least 15 minutes to set.

10. The pops are now ready to eat – just defrost for about 10 minutes before enjoying. Or layer between parchment paper in a sealable plastic bag or container, and freeze for up to a couple of months. Alternatively, these can be served completely defrosted and will keep for a day or two covered in the fridge.

NO-BAKE
PIES & TARTS

Decadent Chocolate &
Cherry Tartlets

Chocolate and cherries are a marriage made in heaven. These indulgent little tarts are surprisingly easy to make and will be sure to impress. Don't add the cherries too early or they may sink too deep. Alternatively, they can simply be served on top. Use any remaining Nutella in the Frozen Mocha Chocca Cups (page 144) or Chocolate & Cardamom Cake-in-a-Cup (page 35).

MAKES 4

125g unsalted butter

25g Nutella or similar chocolate hazelnut spread

21 × Chocolate Creme Oreo cookies (about 1½ × 154g packs)

150g dark chocolate (at least 70% cocoa solids)

300ml double cream

1 tsp vanilla extract

1 tbsp coffee liqueur (like Kahlúa or Tia Maria), optional

20 fresh cherries

100ml double cream, to serve

ESSENTIAL KIT:

4 × 11cm round, straight-sided, loose-bottomed tart tins, 2cm deep

1. Arrange the individual tart tins on a small tray and set aside.

2. First, prepare the tart cases. Melt the butter and Nutella in a large saucepan over a low heat, stirring occasionally. Blitz the cookies in a food processor, or seal in a food bag and bash with a rolling pin, until you have fine crumbs. Tip into the melted Nutella mixture and stir to coat evenly. Divide the crumbs equally between the tart tins (allow just under 100g each). Press them firmly into the base and up the sides of the tins, cover with cling film and chill in the fridge for about 15 minutes until firm.

3. Meanwhile, prepare the filling. Snap the chocolate into a large heatproof bowl and pour over the cream, vanilla extract and coffee liqueur (if using). Either melt the chocolate in the microwave in 30-second blasts, stirring between each go, or over a pan of simmering water, shallow enough that the water doesn't touch the bowl. When the chocolate is melted, stir the mixture until smooth and well blended.

4. Transfer the filling to a jug and pour it into the set tart cases, dividing evenly so it comes just to the top. Return to the fridge for 15–20 minutes until the filling is just beginning to set. Then, sit five cherries with stalks upright into the centre of each tart. They should settle into the pillowy chocolate. Return to the fridge for a further hour or until completely set.

5. When ready to serve, softly whip the cream and serve in a small bowl. Leave the tarts in the tins to serve or carefully remove and sit each one on a doily on a small plate. Let the decadence begin!

Mini Pink Grapefruit Meringue Pies

Mini tart cases are readily bought in supermarkets or speciality food stores. They can be filled with many things but the citrusy bite of this pink grapefruit filling with the soft meringue will have you racing back for more. As the meringue contains raw egg whites, it is not advisable for pregnant women, very young children or anyone frail. You can swap the grapefruit for 2 oranges, 3 lemons or 4 limes.

MAKES 24

Finely grated zest and juice of
1 pink grapefruit

75g caster sugar

50g unsalted butter

4 egg yolks

24 shop-bought mini
shortcrust pastry cases

MERINGUE:

2 egg whites

100g caster sugar

ESSENTIAL KIT:

Electric mixer

Piping bag fitted with a plain
1.5cm nozzle or a disposable
piping bag snipped to this size
opening

Blowtorch or grill

1. Set a medium saucepan with about 10cm of water on a medium heat and bring to a simmer. Place the pink grapefruit zest and juice, the sugar, butter and egg yolks into a large heatproof bowl and sit it on the pan of simmering water. Leave to cook and thicken enough to coat the back of a spoon, stirring occasionally. This should take 20–25 minutes.

2. Remove the bowl from the heat, press cling film directly on the surface to prevent a skin from forming and leave to cool.

3. Arrange the pastry cases on a large tray. Once cool, spoon the grapefruit filling into the cases to come just to the tops and set aside. These can be prepared a day in advance, keeping them chilled in the fridge until they are ready for topping and serving. Store in a baking tray that is deep enough to prevent a covering of cling film from sticking to the tops.

4. When ready to serve, prepare the meringue topping. Whisk the egg whites in a medium bowl with an electric mixer until soft peaks form. Add the sugar in a few batches, beating until it dissolves before adding the next, to give a smooth, thick and glossy meringue. Spoon the meringue into the piping bag.

5. Pipe the meringue generously on top of each pie in a decorative fashion to come nearly to the edge and to give about a 3cm-high peak. Use a blowtorch to turn the meringue evenly golden. Alternatively, give them a quick toasting under a hot grill. Arrange on a pretty platter or cake stand and serve immediately. Once topped, these are best eaten within the day.

Green Goddess Pannacotta Pie

Here, creamy pannacotta is used as a luxurious pie filling, in which chocolate and mint combine with a crunchy base to create a really interesting mix of tastes and textures. You can use a sandwich tin if you don't have a pie tin but don't expect the base to reach fully up the sides.

SERVES 8

PIE CRUST:
Sunflower oil, for the tin
75g unsalted butter
6 After Eight mint chocolates
2 × 154g packs Chocolate Creme Oreo cookies

FILLING:
4 gelatine leaves
375ml double cream
375ml whole milk
100g caster sugar
¼ tsp peppermint extract
Green food colouring

TO SERVE:
1 tsp granulated sugar
1 small drop peppermint extract
Green food colouring
12 After Eight mint chocolates
175ml double cream

ESSENTIAL KIT:
18cm pie tin or round sandwich tin

1. Oil the tin and line the base with parchment paper. For the pie crust, place the butter in a medium heatproof bowl and break in 6 After Eights. Either melt in the microwave in 30-second blasts, stirring between each go, or over a pan of simmering water, shallow enough that the water doesn't touch the bowl. Remove from the heat and stir until smooth.

2. Blend the cookies in a food processor, or seal in a food bag and bash with a rolling pin, to fine crumbs. Stir into the melted butter and chocolate to coat evenly and tip into the tin. Using your hands, press it down evenly along the base and up the sides. Cover with cling film and chill for 15 minutes until firm.

3. For the filling, soak the gelatine in a small bowl with enough cold water to cover, for 5–10 minutes until softened. Slowly bring the cream, milk and sugar to the boil in a medium saucepan, stirring occasionally, then remove from the heat. Stir in the peppermint extract, followed by the food colouring, a tiny bit at a time, to give your desired shade. Squeezing off excess water, stir in the softened gelatine until dissolved. Leave to cool to room temperature. Once cool, pour into the firm pie case and chill for at least 3 hours, until set. This can be prepared up to 24 hours in advance.

4. Meanwhile, make mint sugar by mixing the sugar, peppermint extract and a tiny bit of food colouring in a small bowl. Set aside.

5. To serve, break 9 After Eights into a small bowl with 25ml of the cream and melt as before. Whisk the remaining cream in a large bowl to soft peaks. Dollop on top of the pie and drizzle with the melted After Eights. Break the remaining After Eights on top, scatter with the mint sugar and serve.

Deep-Pan Double Chocolate Mousse Pie

Did somebody say 'deep pan', 'double chocolate' and 'mousse pie' all in the same breath? Indeed they did! This clever pie base is created by assembling chocolate Swiss roll slices inside a tin. It looks (and tastes) best when the Swiss roll has a chocolate filling but a creamy vanilla one works fine too. The chocolate mousse can also be made separately and set in pretty cups or glasses. Bear in mind that the mousse contains uncooked eggs, so isn't suitable for pregnant women, very young children or anyone frail.

SERVES 10

Sunflower oil, for greasing

4 gelatine leaves

3 × 270g chocolate Swiss rolls

200g white chocolate

50ml boiling water

3 eggs, separated into 2 large bowls

1 tsp vanilla extract

350ml double cream

1 tsp cocoa powder

Small handful of Chocolate Curls (page 184)

ESSENTIAL KIT:

23cm round, springform cake tin

Electric whisk

15cm-wide paper doily

1. Grease the cake tin with oil and line the sides with parchment paper.

2. Soak the gelatine leaves in a small bowl in just enough cold water to cover, for 5–10 minutes until softened.

3. Cut each Swiss roll into 10 slices, 1.5cm thick, and use about half of them to line the side of the tin, in a single row standing upright and pressed close together. Use the remaining slices to line the bottom of the tin in a single layer, packing them in tightly and filling any gaps with broken-up pieces. Set aside.

4. Snap the chocolate into a small heatproof bowl and either melt in the microwave in 30-second blasts, stirring between each go, or over a pan of simmering water, shallow enough that the water doesn't touch the bowl. Once melted, remove from the heat, stir until smooth and leave to cool to body temperature.

5. Measure the boiling water in a jug. Squeeze the excess water from the now-softened gelatine and stir the gelatine into the boiled water until dissolved. Leave to cool.

6. Beat together the egg yolks and vanilla extract until well blended. Using an electric whisk, beat the egg whites to soft peaks. When you lift some up on the whisk the peak should droop slightly. Finally, whisk the cream to soft peaks in a large bowl.

CONTINUED

↝ *CONTINUED FROM OVERLEAF*

7. Stir the cooled chocolate and gelatine liquid into the egg yolk mixture. Gently fold in the cream, followed by the egg whites, until everything is well combined. Slowly pour the mixture from a low height into the Swiss roll-lined tin, levelling the top with the back of a spoon. Refrigerate for about 3 hours until set. Cling film may stick to the top, so don't worry about covering.

8. When ready to serve, carefully remove the mousse pie from the tin, place on a cake stand and peel off the paper. Lay the paper doily gently on top of the chocolate mousse and dust cocoa powder through a fine sieve all over the top. Carefully lift the doily off – use the tip of a knife to help get a grip on it and, being careful not to tip any cocoa off the paper, lift it straight up and away – to reveal the pretty pattern. Arrange the chocolate curls in the centre and serve. Cut into 10 wedges and indulge.

Fig & Mascarpone Tarts with Orange Syrup

These elegant little tarts are very quick and easy to make. Make sure you buy sweet tart cases rather than savoury, and fill them just before serving to avoid them becoming soggy. You can top the tarts with any fruit and nut combination you like, if fig and pistachio doesn't work for you. The orange syrup is also delicious used as a cordial over ice and topped up with sparkling water.

SERVES 6

500g mascarpone

75g icing sugar

Finely grated zest and juice of 1 orange

Seeds scraped from 1 vanilla pod

6 individual shop-bought sweet pastry cases

50g caster sugar

2 tbsp clear honey

1 cinnamon stick

6 fresh figs

25g shelled green pistachios, roughly chopped

Few small fresh mint sprigs

1. Place the mascarpone in a medium bowl, sift over the icing sugar and add the orange zest and vanilla seeds. Mix everything together until smooth and well blended. This can be prepared up to 24 hours in advance and stored in the fridge.

2. Arrange the pastry cases on a small tray and divide the mascarpone mixture evenly between them. Cover loosely with cling film and chill in the fridge while you make the syrup.

3. Measure the orange juice into a jug and, if necessary, top up with water to make 100ml. Pour into a small saucepan and add the sugar, honey and cinnamon stick. Bring slowly to the boil, stirring, until the sugar dissolves and then reduce to simmer for about 10 minutes until syrupy. Remove from the heat and leave to infuse and cool.

4. When ready to serve, halve a fig from top to bottom and cut each half into three wedges. Arrange the six wedges in a circle on one tart, cut side up and slightly overlapping with the tips pointing inwards. Repeat with the remaining tarts and sit each on a small serving plate. Scatter with chopped pistachios, drizzle each with about 2 teaspoons of orange syrup, decorate with mint and serve.

For an added twist . . .

✶ **Tropical tarts:** Use 2 limes instead of the orange, a bashed lemongrass stalk in place of the cinnamon stick, and top the tarts with fresh mango slices, instead of figs. To serve, omit the pistachios and scatter with toasted desiccated coconut instead.

Teeny White Chocolate, Pistachio & Raspberry Tarts

These go down a treat at any party, whether the room is full of kids or grown-ups. They're perfect for afternoon tea or make a welcome addition to a picnic hamper or lunchbox. They're also gorgeous as a gift. The cases can be prepared and filled ahead of time, leaving you just the final flourishes to add at the last minute.

MAKES 12

75g unsalted butter
100g digestive biscuits
3 tbsp shelled green pistachios
100g white chocolate
50ml double cream
Seeds scraped from 1 vanilla pod
12 fresh raspberries

ESSENTIAL KIT:

12-hole mini muffin tin
12 mini paper muffin cases

1. Line the tin with cases, and line a small tray with parchment paper.

2. Melt the butter in a large saucepan over a low heat. Blitz the biscuits and 2 tablespoons of the pistachios in a food processor, or seal in a food bag and bash with a rolling pin, until you have fine crumbs and finely crushed nuts. Stir into the melted butter to coat well, and divide evenly between the cases. Press the crumbs firmly into the base and up the sides, cover with cling film and chill for about 1 hour, until set firm.

3. About 15 minutes before the cases are ready, prepare the filling. Snap the chocolate into a medium heatproof bowl and add the cream. Either melt in the microwave in 30-second blasts, stirring between each go, or over a pan of simmering water, shallow enough that the water doesn't touch the bowl. Once melted, stir until smooth and add the vanilla seeds. Leave to cool to body temperature.

4. Use the tip of a pointed knife to lift the tarts carefully out of the tin. Gently peel the paper cases away and arrange on the tray. Spoon the filling equally between them and chill for 15 minutes or until the filling is set. These can be prepared a day in advance.

5. When ready to serve, arrange on a pretty tiered cake stand. Sit a raspberry, pointy side up in the centre of each one. Roughly chop the remaining tablespoon of pistachios and scatter over.

For an added twist . . .

★ Substitute the white chocolate with milk or dark.
★ Top with a cherry or strawberry instead of a raspberry.

Banoffee Cornflake Crust Pie

A pie like this is what dreams are made of! The chewy base, luxurious toffee filling and irresistible topping of cream, bananas and crunchy honeycomb tick all the right boxes. You can use a sandwich tin if you don't have a pie tin but don't expect the cornflake crust to reach fully up the sides.

SERVES 6

PIE CRUST:

Sunflower oil, for the tin

200g white mini marshmallows

50g unsalted butter

75g cornflakes

CARAMEL FILLING:

100g caster sugar

1 × 400g can condensed milk

50g unsalted butter

1 tsp sea salt flakes

TOPPING:

150ml double cream

½ tsp ground cinnamon

2 ripe bananas

125g Honeycomb, to decorate (page 187 or shop-bought), optional

ESSENTIAL KIT:

20cm pie tin or round sandwich tin

1. Oil the tin and line the base with parchment paper. To prepare the pie crust, heat the marshmallows and butter in a large saucepan over a low heat for about 5 minutes, stirring frequently, until melted. Sit a tablespoon in a small jug of boiling water. Remove the melted marshmallows from the heat and immediately crumble in the cornflakes, handfuls at a time, and stir until well coated. Working quickly before it sets, spoon the mixture into the tin and spread it out evenly along the base and up the sides with the back of the hot spoon, pressing down well. Set aside.

2. To make the caramel filling, place the sugar and 50ml of water in a medium pan over a low heat, stirring until dissolved. Increase the heat, bring to the boil and leave to bubble for 5 minutes, without stirring, until it turns a dark golden colour. Remove from the heat and add about a quarter of the condensed milk. The mixture will hiss and spit but keep stirring and it will die down. Stir in the remaining condensed milk, followed by the butter and salt. Return to the heat and boil until it forms a smooth, rich toffee sauce.

3. Pour the filling into the set pie crust and leave to cool completely. Chill for about 2 hours until set. Don't cover with cling film as it may stick to the top. This can be prepared a day in advance and left in the fridge.

4. When ready to serve, whisk the cream with half of the ground cinnamon in a medium bowl until softly whipped. Peel and cut the bananas into 1.5cm-thick diagonal slices and arrange them in a pile on top of the toffee filling. Dollop the cream on top and dust with the remaining ground cinnamon, through a fine sieve. Crumble over the honeycomb, if using, and serve at once.

Individual Pecan Pies
with Salted Pretzel Cases

The bases of these pies are made from blitzed pretzels, in which the slight saltiness and crunchiness contrasts beautifully with the rich, smooth toffee filling. The pies make a perfect after-dinner treat that guests won't forget in a hurry! Serve with your choice of cream or crème fraîche.

MAKES 6

CASES:

Sunflower oil, for greasing

150g salted pretzels

150g caster sugar

150g unsalted butter, softened

FILLING:

150g unsalted butter

150g soft dark brown sugar

1 × 400g can condensed milk

Seeds scraped from 1 vanilla pod

300g pecan halves

Honey or maple syrup, to drizzle

ESSENTIAL KIT:

6 individual 10cm round, loose-bottomed, fluted tart tins, 2cm deep

Food processor

1. Lightly grease the tart tins with oil and set aside on a tray.

2. To make the cases, briefly blitz the pretzels and sugar in a food processor to give medium-sized crumbs. Add the butter and blitz again, until combined. Divide the mixture evenly between the tart tins (about 75g each) and line the base and sides with it. Chill in the fridge for 15 minutes to firm up.

3. To make the filling, heat the butter and sugar together in a medium saucepan over a gentle heat, stirring until the butter melts and sugar dissolves. Add the condensed milk and vanilla seeds and, stirring constantly, bring gently just to boiling point and then remove from the heat.

4. Pour into the firm pretzel cases, levelling the tops with the back of a spoon. Arrange the pecans pretty side up, all over the top of each pie. They look nice arranged in rings starting at the outside and working inwards. Cover with cling film and chill in the fridge for 30 minutes or overnight, until firm to the touch.

5. To serve, remove each pie carefully from its tin and arrange in the centre of a small serving plate. Drizzle the pecans with a little honey or maple syrup for a glazed finish.

For an added twist. . .

★ Turn this into a banoffee pie by swapping the pecans for banana slices and topping with cream.

NO-BAKE
SWEET TREATS

Peppermint Cream Buttons

With their minty-fresh flavour and unique texture, peppermint creams are very addictive. These look attractive displayed in a glass jar as a gift. The world is your oyster when it comes to button designs, or just make simple rounds. Be sure to use paste food colours rather than liquids as they don't make the mixture so wet.

MAKES about 35 of various sizes

450g icing sugar

175ml condensed milk

¼ tsp peppermint extract, or to taste

Selection of 5 paste food colourings of your choice

ESSENTIAL KIT:

7.5cm, 6cm and 2.5cm round, straight-sided cutters

3cm flower-shaped cutter

Selection of bottle caps, glasses or jars

Wooden skewer

Large wire cooling rack

1. Cut out ten 15cm squares of parchment paper, and also line a large tray with parchment. Sift the icing sugar into a large bowl and stir in the condensed milk and peppermint extract to form a soft dough. Add more peppermint to taste.

2. Place five equal batches (each about 120g) on paper squares. Cover all but one with cling film to prevent drying out. Add a small dot of food colouring to this one and knead until evenly blended, wearing disposable or rubber gloves to avoid dying your hands. Repeat until you reach your desired shade. Do the same for the other batches, using a different colour each time.

3. Lay another paper square on top of each batch and roll out to about 5mm thick. Working with one batch at a time and keeping the others covered in the fridge, stamp out any sizes and shapes you like (or for 35 pieces, cut one large, two medium and two small rounds, and two flowers from each batch). Re-roll as necessary and arrange on the lined tray as you go.

4. Fashion into buttons by pressing the flat side of a bottle cap lightly into the centre to make a dip, or using the other side for a thin rim. Alternatively, use the rim of a glass or jar that fits the button. With the wooden skewer, pierce two or four holes in the centre, and crimp the edges with a fork or the tip of a sharp knife. If they become too soft, return to the fridge to firm up. Arrange on parchment paper on the wire rack as you go.

5. When finished, leave for at least 12 hours or overnight to dry out. These keep for up to a week, layered between parchment paper in an airtight container.

Strawberry & Mascarpone Pancake Swirligigs

These are a lovely 'twist' on baked treats like palmiers and pastry swirls. Made from pancakes topped with a delicious filling then rolled up and sliced, they sit perfectly on any party table or in a picnic box. They are also an easy but impressive breakfast treat for guests. If this recipe makes more than you need, freeze half the pancakes for another time and halve the filling quantities.

MAKES 48 slices

PANCAKES:

125g plain flour

225ml whole milk

1 egg

25g unsalted butter

MASCARPONE FILLING:

50g Strawberry Purée (page 185)

250g mascarpone

25g icing sugar

50g fresh strawberries, hulled and finely chopped

ESSENTIAL KIT:

20cm non-stick crepe or frying pan

1. Line a large tray with parchment paper and set aside.

2. Tip the flour into a large jug, make a well in the centre and add the milk and egg. Whisk everything together until smooth and well blended. Leave aside to rest for a few minutes.

3. Meanwhile, prepare the filling. If you haven't already, make the strawberry purée. Beat the mascarpone in a medium bowl to loosen. Sift in the icing sugar, add the strawberry purée and beat well to combine. Add the chopped strawberries and stir gently. Cover with cling film and chill until needed.

4. To make the pancakes, warm the frying pan over a medium heat and add a quarter of the butter. Once melted, ladle in a quarter of the pancake mix (about 100ml) and swirl the pan to spread it evenly around. Cook for 1–2 minutes each side until golden brown and cooked through. Remove the pancake and lay it flat on the prepared tray and repeat to make another three. Leave until completely cool.

5. To assemble, spread a quarter of the mascarpone filling evenly over each pancake. Roll each one up tightly like you would a Swiss roll to enclose the filling. Wrap each one individually in cling film and chill in the fridge for at least 1 hour or until firm. These can be made up to 24 hours in advance.

6. When ready to serve, unwrap the cling film and, using a sharp knife, cut each roll into 12 slices, 1.5cm thick, giving 48 in total. Arrange in concentric circles on a large round platter and serve. These will keep for a couple of days covered in the fridge.

Toastie Triangles with Creamy Lemon Filling

Who'd have thought you can create baked goodies in a sandwich toaster? You need one with triangular moulds here, rather than a café-style panini press. These also work well on a waffle maker: for an 11cm square waffle plate use 100g of the mix, and serve with the filling piled on top.

MAKES 8

CAKES:

175g unsalted butter, roughly chopped

175g golden caster sugar

150g self-raising flour

100g ground almonds

1 tsp baking powder

150g natural yoghurt

3 eggs

Seeds scraped from ½ vanilla pod

Sunflower oil, for greasing

1 tsp icing sugar

FILLING:

250g mascarpone

50g natural yoghurt

Seeds scraped from ½ vanilla pod

75g lemon curd

ESSENTIAL KIT:

Toasted sandwich maker (or waffle maker, see intro)

1. First, prepare the filling. Beat the mascarpone and yoghurt in a medium bowl to loosen. Beat in the vanilla seeds and barely stir in the lemon curd to give a rippled effect. Cover with cling film and chill until serving.

2. For the cake mix, melt the butter in a small pan on the hob or a bowl in the microwave. Remove from the heat and let cool a little.

3. Toss the sugar, flour, ground almonds and baking powder together in a large bowl and make a well in the centre.

4. Place the yoghurt, eggs and vanilla seeds in a medium bowl and pour in the melted butter. Whisk until well combined and pour into the dry ingredients. Fold together until well mixed.

5. Lightly grease the toastie maker with oil on kitchen paper and turn it on. When ready, spoon mixture into each triangle until level with the top. Close the lid and cook for 2–3 minutes until golden brown underneath. Using a heatproof spatula and working quickly but carefully, flip it over and cook on the other side, with the lid down, for a further 2 minutes until a skewer inserted into the centre comes out clean. Remove carefully and repeat to get 16 in total. You may need to re-grease a few times – be careful as the plates are now hot.

6. These are best served warm, but not too hot or the filling will melt. Spread the filling evenly over half of the cake triangles, then pop the remaining half on as lids. Arrange on a long platter slightly overlapping each other. Dust with icing sugar and serve.

Kataifi Bananas with Ginger & Honey Syrup

Kataifi pastry is a finely shredded filo pastry widely used in Middle Eastern, Greek and Turkish cooking, particularly for sweet treats. You can buy it in the freezer section of good Asian stores (or use regular filo pastry if you can't find it). These make a beautiful dessert served with vanilla ice cream. Leftover syrup can be kept in a sealed bottle in the fridge and used as a cordial, mixed with boiling water for a winter tonic or drizzled over fresh fruits or ice cream.

MAKES 16

150ml clear honey

50g golden caster sugar

2.5cm piece of fresh ginger, peeled and finely grated

Sunflower oil, for deep frying

2 tbsp plain flour

1 egg

125g kataifi pastry, defrosted

2 bananas

ESSENTIAL KIT:

Frying/sugar thermometer (if you have one)

1. Place the honey and sugar in a small saucepan with 150ml of water and slowly bring to the boil, stirring until the sugar dissolves. Once boiled, reduce the heat and add the ginger. Simmer for 5 minutes until reduced and thickened. Remove from the heat and leave to infuse and thicken further on cooling.

2. Warm 10cm depth of oil in a wide, heavy-based saucepan over a medium heat. Be very careful as the oil will become extremely hot.

3. Scatter the flour on a small plate and beat the egg in a small bowl. Gently pull the pastry into 16 even-sized piles, arranging them on a clean surface. Peel the bananas and cut each lengthways in half and then widthways into quarters to give 16 pieces. Toss the banana pieces in the flour to coat, then in the egg and finally sit one on each pastry nest. Wrap the pastry up around to enclose.

4. If you have a thermometer to check the oil, the perfect cooking temperature is 160°C. If not, test if the oil is ready by dropping in a small ball of kataifi pastry – it should gently sizzle and take 1–2 minutes to turn golden brown. Once ready, work in batches to fry the banana rolls for about 3 minutes, turning halfway through, until crisp and golden brown. If the rolls begin to burn, either turn down the heat or pour a little more room-temperature oil into the pan.

5. Drain the kataifi bananas on kitchen paper and arrange on a serving platter or tray. Strain the ginger and honey syrup through a fine sieve into a small bowl, place on the platter for dipping and serve. These are best eaten straight away.

Shiny Indian Diamonds

India has a delicious array of confectionery and these diamonds are a variation on a traditional treat called barfi, with a base of cashew nuts and almonds, and flavoured with cardamom and rosewater. You can vary the spices, using cinnamon and mixed spice if you prefer. Silver (and gold) edible leaf can be found in some supermarkets and online, else dust the top with edible lustre or icing sugar.

MAKES 27 (+ about 15 offcuts)

Sunflower oil, for greasing

125g unsalted cashew nuts

400g golden caster sugar

125g ground almonds

2 tbsp whole milk

½ tsp ground cardamom

1 tsp rosewater

8 × 8cm square sheets of edible silver leaf

ESSENTIAL KIT:

20cm square cake tin

Food processor

1. Grease the cake tin with oil and line with parchment paper, leaving 5cm excess hanging over the sides to help with lifting out later.

2. Blend the cashew nuts in a food processor until finely ground. Tip into a large saucepan and add the sugar, ground almonds, milk, ground cardamom and rosewater. Cook on a low heat, stirring constantly, for 8–10 minutes until it forms a dough which comes away from the sides of the pan.

3. Spread the dough evenly in the prepared tin, smoothing it out with your hands or the back of a spoon. Leave to cool and then cover with cling film and chill in the fridge for at least 1 hour until set. This can be made a couple of days in advance and kept in the fridge.

4. When ready to serve, lift out of the tin and peel off the paper. Very carefully, lay the squares of silver foil in a single layer all over the top. They can blow around quite easily so work slowly and use a clean, dry pastry brush to coax them into place.

5. To cut the diamonds, place the slab on a board and, using a long, sharp knife, cut in half diagonally. Then, moving along 2.5cm each time, make cuts parallel with the first cut, to create 10 strips in total. Now with the slab sitting square to you, cut it vertically into seven 2.5cm-wide strips. This will produce 27 whole diamonds (and about 15 not-quite diamond shapes).

6. Arrange on a cake stand and serve. These can be stored for up to a week, layered between sheets of parchment paper in an airtight container in the fridge.

Coconut & Lime Paradise Eggs

These morsels of coconut and lime will transport your tastebuds to tropical climes! You can coat them entirely in chocolate (using double the quantity specified) for the ultimate 'died and went to heaven' effect. Virgin coconut oil is available in many supermarkets and health-food stores and has various health benefits. These eggs are gluten free and can be vegan if you use agave nectar instead of honey.

MAKES 12

200g desiccated coconut

3 tbsp boiling water

4 tbsp virgin coconut oil

Seeds scraped from 1 vanilla pod

Finely grated zest and juice of 2 limes

100g clear honey

4 tbsp coconut milk

150g dark chocolate (at least 70% cocoa solids)

ESSENTIAL KIT:

Food processor

1. Line a large tray that will fit in the freezer with parchment paper.

2. Soak the coconut in the boiling water for 10 minutes, until absorbed. Blend in a food processor, with the coconut oil, for 1 minute to make a crumbly mixture. Add the vanilla seeds, lime zest and juice, honey and coconut milk. Blend again until well combined.

3. Divide the mixture into 12 even-sized pieces. The easiest way to do this is simply to weigh the whole mixture and then divide it by 12 to give you the required weight of each piece – then weigh as you go. Squeezing firmly with your hands, bring the mixture together and mould it into an egg shape, then lay each one on the prepared tray. Cover with cling film and freeze for 1 hour until firm. These can be prepared in advance and kept in the freezer for a few months.

4. Once firm, snap the chocolate into a small heatproof bowl. Either melt in the microwave in 30-second blasts, stirring between each go, or over a pan of simmering water, shallow enough that the water doesn't touch the bowl. When melted, remove from the heat and leave to cool to body temperature for a few minutes.

5. Carefully hold the pointy end of an egg and dip the base into the melted chocolate, tilting the bowl a little to pool it, so it comes halfway up the sides. Lay the egg back on the tray and repeat with all the others. Chill in the fridge for 30 minutes until the chocolate is set, by which stage the eggs will have defrosted enough for eating.

6. These eggs look great presented in a cardboard egg box. They will keep for up to a week in an airtight container in the fridge.

Chocolate Peanut Butter Cups

These little tasties are a take on the iconic Reese's peanut butter cups that are loved in the USA. It's best to use silicone cupcake cases here, if you have them, as it is easier to pop the cups out of silicone than paper cases (although paper is fine if that's all you have). These are best served straight from the fridge.

MAKES 12

100g dark chocolate (at least 70% cocoa solids)

300g milk chocolate

40g icing sugar

150g smooth peanut butter

2 tsp unsalted butter, softened

ESSENTIAL KIT:

12-hole muffin tin

12 silicone or paper cupcake cases

1. Line the muffin tin with the cupcake cases.

2. Snap half of each of the chocolates into a large heatproof bowl and melt either in the microwave in 30-second blasts, stirring between each go, or over a pan of simmering water, shallow enough that the water doesn't touch the bowl. Once melted, remove from the heat.

3. Divide the melted chocolate evenly between the cupcake cases, about 1cm deep. Gently bang the tin on the work surface to level the chocolate out. Leave to cool, then cover with cling film and chill in the fridge for 30 minutes until firm.

4. Once they are set, sift the icing sugar into a large bowl, add the peanut butter and butter and beat together until smooth. Divide this evenly between the cupcake cases, spreading it level with the back of a teaspoon. Cover and return to the fridge for 5–10 minutes, while you prepare the final layer.

5. Snap the remaining dark and milk chocolates into the chocolate bowl and melt as before. Remove from the heat and leave to cool to body temperature. Then divide the melted chocolate evenly on top of the peanut butter, levelling the tops if necessary. Cover and chill in the fridge for at least 30 minutes or until set hard.

6. Pop them out of the cupcake cases and dive in! Any survivors will keep for up to a week in an airtight container in the fridge.

Doughnut Cake Pops

Not only do these super-cute cake pops have very few ingredients, they are also easy-peasy to make, so are ideal for kids to help out with, especially the shaping and decorating part. Serve these at parties or wrapped in pretty packaging as a lovely gift. They can easily be shaped into balls if you prefer.

MAKES 16

2 × 154g packs Oreo cookies

100g full-fat cream cheese

100g white chocolate

½ tsp each of four types of edible sprinkles

Milk, to serve, optional

ESSENTIAL KIT:

Food processor

16 × 20cm lollipop sticks

1. Line a large tray with parchment paper.

2. Blend the Oreo cookies to fine crumbs in a food processor. Add the cream cheese and blend again to give a really smooth and shiny dough mixture. Divide the mixture into 16 equal-sized pieces (weighing about 25g each).

3. Shape one piece into a ball and flatten it slightly between the palms of your hands. Lay it on the prepared tray and use the end of a wooden spoon handle to punch a hole in the centre. Repeat with all the pieces. Cover with cling film and chill for about 2 hours until firm.

4. Once they are firm, snap the white chocolate into a small heatproof bowl and either melt in the microwave in 30-second blasts, stirring between each go, or over a pan of simmering water, shallow enough that the water doesn't touch the bowl. When melted, remove from the heat and leave to cool to body temperature.

5. Dip a lollipop stick about 1cm into the melted chocolate and allow the excess to drip off. Then insert this part of the stick into the side of a doughnut, without allowing it to break through to the centre. The chocolate will set and glue the stick in place. Then, with the cake pop lying down, carefully spoon a teaspoon of the melted chocolate over the top, allowing it to dribble a little down the edges to give that classic iced doughnut look. Scatter with a pinch of edible sprinkles. Repeat with the remaining cake pops and then chill in the fridge for 30 minutes until completely set.

6. These are fun served standing upright in small glass bottles of milk. Alternatively, stand them in bunches in tall glasses to serve. They can be stored for a couple of days covered in the fridge.

Choco-Mallow Tea Cakes

These are so retro! With a crumbly biscuit base, crisp chocolate coating and a soft mallowy centre with a jammy surprise, you won't be able to resist eating more than one! You can omit the jam if you prefer or spread a little Salted Caramel Sauce (page 182) or dulce de leche caramel on the biscuit instead. As the mallow here is not fully cooked these are not suitable for pregnant women, very young children or anyone frail.

MAKES 28

28 × 5cm round plain (or chocolate) biscuits

100g raspberry jam

200g caster sugar

3 egg whites

½ tsp cream of tartar

1 tsp vanilla extract

500g plain chocolate (at least 70% cocoa solids)

ESSENTIAL KIT:

Electric handheld whisk

Piping bag with a 1.5cm plain nozzle or a disposable piping bag snipped to this size

1. Lay the biscuits out on a wire rack and spoon a small teaspoon of the jam in the centre of each one.

2. Place the sugar, egg white, cream of tartar, vanilla extract and 50ml of water into a medium heatproof bowl and beat with an electric handheld whisk for a minute until the mixture turns opaque. Sit the bowl on top of a pan of simmering water, shallow enough that the water doesn't touch the bowl. Using the electric whisk, beat the mixture for 5–6 minutes until it doubles in volume, becomes thick and glossy and can form stiff peaks. Remove from the heat, spoon into the piping bag and pipe a 4cm-high peaked dome on top of the jam on each biscuit, to come nearly to the edge. Pop the tray into the fridge for 20 minutes so the mallow firms up a little.

3. Meanwhile, snap the chocolate into a medium heatproof bowl and either melt in the microwave in 30-second blasts, stirring between each go, or over a pan of simmering water, shallow enough that the water doesn't touch the bowl. When melted, remove from the heat and leave to cool to body temperature.

4. When everything is ready, hold a tea cake over the bowl of melted chocolate and spoon generously with chocolate to coat all over. Return to the rack and repeat for all. Chill in the fridge for 30 minutes until set firm. These will keep for a couple of days in the fridge. Nibble on them at your pleasure!

Sweet Cinnamon & Ricotta Tortilla Triangles

These unique little treats are a divine mix of sweet and savoury. Tortilla wraps tend to be used for savoury dishes but in fact they make the perfect carrier for this yummy blend of ricotta, cinnamon, raisins and walnuts. The triangles have a freshly baked feel to them even though they are cooked in a frying pan. Alternatively, they can be cooked one at a time on a panini-style sandwich toaster, for 2–3 minutes in total.

MAKES 8

25g Caramelised Walnuts (page 182), roughly chopped

125g ricotta cheese

25g raisins, roughly chopped

4 tsp clear honey

25g unsalted butter, softened

¼ tsp ground cinnamon

2 large flour tortillas

1. Prepare the caramelised walnuts, if you haven't already done so.

2. To prepare the ricotta filling, mix the ricotta, raisins and honey in a medium bowl and set aside.

3. Lay out two separate pieces of parchment paper at least the size of a tortilla. Put a large, dry frying pan (at least as wide as one tortilla) on a medium heat. Mix the butter and cinnamon together in a small bowl and spread it evenly on one side of each tortilla. Flip each one over onto its piece of parchment paper, buttered-side down. Spread the ricotta mixture over half of each tortilla with the back of a spoon. Scatter the chopped walnuts over the ricotta. Finally, fold each tortilla over to encase the filling.

4. Slide the tortillas off the paper and into the pan together, straight folded sides back to back. Cook gently on each side for 2–3 minutes until lightly toasted, squishing them down a bit with a fish slice as they cook.

5. Slide them out of the pan, cut each into four wedges and serve piled up on a pretty plate. These are best eaten warm and fresh.

NO-BAKE
ICED DREAMS

Banana Split Sundae Kamikaze Cake

Kids and adults alike will be wowed by this over-the-top ice-cream cake. For speed, use shop-bought ice cream or prepare homemade versions well in advance. When decorating, take inspiration from retro ice-cream parlours and go mad with sprinkles, sauces or anything you fancy. Maraschino cherries with stems really are the cherry on the cake (see page 96 for more details).

SERVES 12

Sunflower oil, for greasing

650ml each of Raspberry, Chocolate and Vanilla Ice Cream (pages 184–5 or shop-bought)

350g Raspberry Purée (page 185)

75g unsalted butter

2 × 154g packs Chocolate Creme Oreo cookies

6 bananas

250ml Chocolate Sauce (page 183), at room temperature

150ml double cream

12 wafer cigar rolls

12 maraschino cherries (with stems if possible)

2 tbsp edible sprinkles

ESSENTIAL KIT:

20cm round, springform cake tin, at least 9cm deep

Regular or disposable piping bag set with a star nozzle

1. Grease the cake tin with oil and line the sides with parchment paper. Choose a small deep tray that will fit in the freezer and line with parchment paper.

2. Remove all three ice creams from the freezer and leave to soften enough for scooping. Make the raspberry purée, if you haven't already.

3. Meanwhile, melt the butter in a medium saucepan on the hob or in a bowl in the microwave. Blend the Oreo cookies in a food processor, or seal them in a food bag and bash with a rolling pin, until you have fine crumbs. Mix the crumbs into the melted butter until well coated and spread evenly into the base of the tin with the back of a spoon.

4. Peel and cut two of the bananas into 1cm-thick slices and arrange in a single layer on top of the base. Spoon over a third of the raspberry purée, spreading it out evenly and then cover with cling film. Pop into the freezer for about 15 minutes to firm up the base.

5. Scoop three balls (about 50g each) from each ice-cream flavour and arrange them spaced apart on the prepared tray. Cover with cling film and place in the freezer until ready to serve. Continue to leave the remaining ice cream to soften further until spreadable.

6. When ready, spread the raspberry ice cream all over the set base first. Peel the remaining bananas, slice as before and lay half of

CONTINUED

➡️ *CONTINUED FROM OVERLEAF*

them in an even layer on top. Spoon another third of the raspberry purée over, spreading it out evenly. Next evenly spread with the chocolate ice cream, followed by the remaining bananas and purée, and finish with the vanilla ice cream. Cover with cling film and pop into the freezer for at least 8 hours or overnight, until frozen solid.

7. Before serving, make the chocolate sauce, if you haven't already. Pour into a serving jug and leave to cool to room temperature.

8. To serve, remove the cake from the tin, sitting it on a cake stand or serving plate. Peel the parchment paper from the sides and then leave for 15–20 minutes to soften a little.

9. Meanwhile, whip the cream until just stiff and spoon it into the piping bag. Pipe all but the final 6 or 7cm of cream into a serving bowl. Arrange the wafer cigar rolls on a small serving plate and the maraschino cherries and edible sprinkles into serving bowls.

10. Here comes the kamikaze bit! Arrange the reserved frozen balls of ice cream in a pile on top of the cake. Gradually pour about a quarter of the chocolate sauce over the scoops, allowing it to drip down. Pipe the reserved cream in a rosette shape between the ice-cream scoops and sit one of the cherries on top. Stick two wafer cigars into the cream and scatter a teaspoon of the sprinkles all over the top. Serve at once with the remaining cream, chocolate sauce, cherries, wafer cigars and sprinkles for everyone to help themselves to. Cut into 12 pieces. This is best done with a long sharp knife which has been dipped in boiling water and wiped dry between each cut.

11. Any leftover ice-cream cake should be frozen straight away. Wrap individual portions in parchment paper and place in a sealable food bag. These will keep happily in the freezer for a few months to enjoy as you please.

Retro & Soul Arctic Roll

Here's a fresh take on the very retro Arctic roll, which will conjure up fond memories for many. The jam and coconut coating is an extra twist that makes the turned-out cake look more attractive (and taste really good!) but you can omit this if you prefer. Strawberry or raspberry ice cream is also delicious instead of vanilla.

SERVES 8

500ml Vanilla Ice Cream (page 184 or shop-bought)

2 × 280g shop-bought Madeira cakes

250g fresh raspberries

50g desiccated coconut

100g raspberry jam

ESSENTIAL KIT:

900g loaf tin (roughly 23cm × 9cm, and 7.5cm deep)

1. Remove the ice cream from the freezer and leave to soften until just spreadable but not completely thawed.

2. Meanwhile, line the tin with a double layer of cling film leaving about 10cm excess hanging over the edges. Trim the ends off the cake slabs and cut each one into eight slices, about 1.5cm thick. Arrange four or five along each side of the tin, and then two or three in the bottom, breaking up to fit if necessary.

3. Lightly crush the raspberries with a fork and set aside about a quarter for the top. Use your hands to spread the rest all over the cake layer. Spoon the softened ice cream into the tin, levelling it off. Spread the remaining raspberries on top and arrange the remaining cake slices on top of that, pressing them down well. Cover with the excess cling film and freeze for at least 8 hours or overnight until frozen solid. This can be prepared up to a few months ahead.

4. Before serving, toast the coconut in a dry frying pan over a medium heat, tossing occasionally until light golden. Remove from the heat and leave to cool until serving.

5. When ready to serve, open up the cling film, place an upturned rectangular plate on top and turn the whole thing over. Lift off the tin and peel off the cling film. Spread the jam on thickly and evenly and stick the coconut all over. Serve immediately. Using a long sharp knife dipped in boiling water and wiped dry each time, cut into eight chunky slices.

6. Freeze any leftovers straight away. Wrap individual portions in parchment paper and seal in a food bag. These will keep happily in the freezer for a few months.

Frozen Yoghurt Breakfast Ring

Make breakfast memorable with this frozen ring of deliciousness, packed with yoghurt, berries and muesli to see you through the morning. Of course it can also be enjoyed at any time of the day. If you don't have a suitable jelly mould, use a loaf or cake tin of the same volume (these alternatives need to be lined with cling film). Feel free to experiment with your favourite yoghurt flavours and fruits.

SERVES 8

300g natural yoghurt

1 × 400g can condensed milk

300g frozen berries, such as fruits of the forest, strawberries or raspberries

200g granola, broken up if in clusters

125g fresh mixed berries

Small handful of fresh mint sprigs

ESSENTIAL KIT:

1.5-litre ring jelly mould

1. Divide both the yoghurt and the condensed milk equally between two separate medium bowls and stir until well blended.

2. Stir the frozen berries into one of the mixes and pour this into the mould, spreading it out evenly.

3. Scatter the granola evenly on top and gently pour the second yoghurt mixture over it, levelling with the back of a spoon.

4. Cover with the lid or cling film and freeze for at least 8 hours or overnight, until frozen solid.

5. Before serving, remove from the freezer and leave to stand for 5–10 minutes to soften a little. Take the cover off and place a round cake stand or serving plate upside down on top. Turn both over together, allowing the ice-cream ring to drop onto the stand and lift off the mould to reveal it. Scatter with the fresh berries and mint sprigs to decorate and serve at once, cutting it into eight portions.

6. Any leftover ice-cream ring should be frozen straight away. Store individual portions in lidded plastic tubs in the freezer, where they will keep happily for a few months to enjoy as you please.

Frozen Mocha Chocca Cups

Blended waffle cones form the cases for these cute ice-cream cupcakes. They are filled with chocolate spread and coffee ice cream, but you can use any fillings you like. The bases can be made in advance and frozen for up to three months – remove from the freezer about 10 minutes before needed so they can soften a bit.

MAKES 4

400ml Coffee Ice Cream (pages 184–5 or shop-bought)

50g Caramelised Pecan Nuts (page 182)

75g unsalted butter

150g waffle ice-cream cones

100ml double cream

1 tbsp coffee liqueur (like Kahlúa or Tia Maria), optional

1 tsp icing sugar

150g Nutella or similar chocolate hazelnut spread

1 tsp instant coffee powder

Small handful of Chocolate Curls (page 184)

ESSENTIAL KIT:

Muffin tin

4 paper muffin cases

Food processor

1. Line four holes in the muffin tin with cases. Choose a small, deep tray that will fit in the freezer and line with parchment paper.

2. Take the ice cream out of the freezer and leave to soften enough for scooping. Make the caramelised nuts, if you haven't already.

3. To make the cups, melt the butter in a medium saucepan or in a bowl in the microwave. In a food processor, blend the waffle cones and half the caramelised nuts to fine crumbs. Tip into the melted butter and stir until well coated. Divide equally between the cases and press into the base and up the sides evenly. Cover with cling film and freeze for about 30 minutes until firm.

4. Scoop the ice cream into eight even balls (about 4cm diameter). Arrange on the prepared tray, cover and freeze until needed. Softly whip the cream in a medium bowl with the coffee liqueur, if using, and sifted icing sugar. Cover and chill until needed.

5. To assemble, divide 100g of Nutella between the set cups. Soften the remaining Nutella in a small bowl in the microwave for 30 seconds or a small pan on a low heat. Meanwhile, place two ice-cream balls in each wafer cup. Drizzle with the melted Nutella and dollop on the whipped cream. Dust with coffee powder, crumble over the remaining caramelised nuts and top with chocolate curls. Serve at once.

For an added twist . . .

★ **Minty choc-chip cups:** Line cases with blended choc-chip cookies instead of wafer cones. Crumble a chocolate brownie into them rather than Nutella, follow with mint ice cream and top with whipped cream and a dusting of cocoa powder.

Watermelon Bombe

Guests won't believe their eyes when this kitsch creation emerges from your freezer! Kids love it – and they'll be even more excited if you let them help. It is best to use bowls from a nesting set so that the layers are even. If making your own mint ice cream, aim for a strong green shade, or if the shop-bought is very pale, boost it with food colouring. There are several stages of freezing here, so allow yourself plenty of time.

SERVES 12

800ml Mint Ice Cream (page 184 or shop-bought)

Sunflower oil, for greasing

200g unsalted butter

400g pink wafer biscuits

1 litre raspberry sorbet

100g small chocolate chips

Sparklers to decorate, optional

ESSENTIAL KIT:

From a set of bowls that nestle inside each other:

2.5 litre bowl (roughly 23cm across the top, 13cm deep)

2.2-litre bowl (roughly 20cm across the top, 10cm deep)

1. Remove the mint ice cream from the freezer and leave to soften until spreadable but not completely thawed.

2. Lightly grease the inside of the large bowl with oil and line with a double layer of cling film, leaving about 15cm excess hanging over the rim. Lightly grease the outside of the smaller bowl with oil and wrap it with a double layer of cling film, leaving a good excess hanging inside the bowl.

3. Once soft, spoon the ice cream into the larger bowl. Sit the smaller bowl inside and press it down gently until the ice cream comes up the sides to about 1.5cm from the top. Cover the exposed ice cream with the excess cling film and freeze for at least 4 hours or until set solid. This stage can be done well ahead of time.

4. Once the ice cream is set, prepare the biscuit layer. Melt the butter in a medium saucepan on the hob or in a bowl in the microwave. Blend the wafer biscuits in a food processor, or seal them in a food bag and bash with a rolling pin, until you have rough crumbs. Mix the biscuit crumbs into the melted butter until well coated.

5. Remove the smaller bowl from the ice-cream bombe, using the inner excess cling film to help pull it up. If very stuck, pour a little boiling water into the small bowl, briefly swirl it around and tip it out. Working quickly before the biscuits set (or the ice cream melts!), press the crumbs evenly all over the inside of the mint ice cream. Cover with cling film and freeze for 15 minutes until set.

CONTINUED

CONTINUED FROM OVERLEAF

6. Meanwhile, remove the raspberry sorbet from the freezer and leave to soften until spreadable. Once soft, stir the chocolate chips evenly through. Spoon this on top of the set crumbs in the bombe, to come to the same level as the top of the ice cream, and smooth with the back of a spoon. Cover with the excess cling film and freeze for at least 4 hours or overnight until frozen solid. This can be prepared up to a few months in advance.

7. Remove from the freezer and briefly run hot water over the outside of the bowl to help loosen the bombe. Open up the cling film and lay a round cake stand or serving plate upside down on top. Turn both over together and then lift the bowl off. Peel the cling film off to reveal the bombe and serve straight away. This looks fun and adds drama when served with lit sparklers on top. Cut into quarters and then each piece into 3 wedges to give 12 in total. This is best done with a long sharp knife, dipped in boiling water and wiped dry between each cut.

8. Any leftover bombe should be frozen straight away. Wrap individual portions in parchment paper and seal in a food bag. These will keep happily in the freezer for a few months to enjoy as you please.

Banana & Toffee Waffle Freezer Cake

The banana ice cream in this cake is ridiculously easy to make, with just ONE ingredient (can you guess what?)! Or try adding a little peanut butter when blending. Stockpile overripe bananas from your fruit bowl, peeled in food bags in the freezer. When you've collected enough, it's your cue to make this cake!

SERVES 8

10 ripe bananas

Sunflower oil, for greasing

6 toffee waffle biscuits

300ml Pecan Caramel Sauce (page 182)

ESSENTIAL KIT:

20cm round, springform cake tin

Food processor

1. Peel the bananas, pop in a food bag and freeze for at least 8 hours or overnight, until solid. When ready to assemble, remove the bananas from the freezer and leave for 20 minutes to soften up.

2. Meanwhile, grease the tin with oil and line with parchment paper. Quarter the waffles and then cut each piece in half again.

3. Blend the slightly soft bananas in a food processor until completely smooth and creamy. Spoon a third of the mix into the tin, spreading evenly. Arrange 28–30 waffle pieces upright around the edge of the tin, sliding them down through the mixture to touch the bottom. To fit them snugly and make a nice pattern, alternate pieces pointing downwards and upwards, until the ring is complete. Reserve the remaining waffle pieces in an airtight container for serving. Pour the rest of the ice cream into the tin and spread evenly. Cover with cling film and freeze for at least 8 hours or overnight, until solid. This can be prepared up to a few months in advance.

4. When ready to serve, remove from the tin and place on a stand. Peel off the paper and sit for about 20 minutes to soften a little. If you haven't already done so, make the pecan caramel sauce and leave to cool. Spreading it out in a wide dish will speed up this process.

5. Pour the cooled sauce all over the top of the cake. Insert the reserved waffle pieces into the top or scatter them over and serve at once. Using a long sharp knife, dipped in boiling water and wiped dry between slices, cut into eight wedges.

6. Any leftovers should be frozen straight away. Wrap individual portions in parchment paper and freeze in a sealed food bag for up to a few months.

Minty Fresh Alaska Iceberg

Baked Alaska is always a showstopper and this is no exception. The cakey texture of the ice-cream sandwiches will have people baffled as to how you made it without an oven. You can find ice-cream sandwiches in many supermarkets. The meringue layer here is toasted rather than fully cooked – it's totally delicious but not suitable for very young children, pregnant women or anyone frail.

SERVES 10

750ml Mint Ice Cream (page 184 or shop-bought)

8 × 100ml rectangular ice-cream sandwiches (ideally 13cm × 4.5cm but see Essential kit)

5 egg whites

275g caster sugar

1 tsp white wine vinegar

¼ tsp peppermint extract

ESSENTIAL KIT:

900g loaf tin (about 23cm × 10cm or roughly twice the length and width of your ice-cream sandwiches)

Heatproof and freezer-proof serving plate (slightly longer and wider than the loaf tin)

Food mixer

Piping bag with plain 1.5cm nozzle or disposable piping bag snipped to this size opening

Blowtorch or grill

1. Allow the mint ice cream to soften until easily spreadable. Meanwhile, line the tin with a double layer of cling film, allowing a 10cm excess to hang over the edges.

2. Once soft, spoon the ice cream into the tin, compact it down and spread it out evenly with the back of a spoon. Cover with the excess cling film and freeze for 1–2 hours until frozen solid. This can be prepared up to a few months in advance.

3. When ready to assemble, lay two ice-cream sandwiches beside each other at one end of the serving plate, with the rectangles pointing in the same direction as the plate. Follow with another two sandwiches on the other half of the plate. Unwrap the frozen mint ice-cream block and sit it on top. Arrange the remaining four ice-cream sandwiches on top of that. Cover and return to the freezer.

4. Whisk the egg whites in a food mixer until soft peaks form. Gradually add the sugar in stages, continuing to whisk. Add the vinegar and peppermint extract and continue to whisk until really stiff and glossy. Spoon into the piping bag, which you may have to refill once or twice. Pipe meringue peaks in neat rows all over the sides and top of the ice-cream loaf. Alternatively, simply spread it on with a palette knife, creating whatever pattern you like.

5. Use a blowtorch to brown the meringue all over or toast briefly under a hot grill. Serve at once, decorated with pretty bunting if you like. Cut into 10 even-sized slices. This is best done with a long sharp knife, dipped in boiling water and wiped dry between each cut. The meringue doesn't freeze well so this is best eaten on the same day.

Dime Bar Bombe with Millionaire's Drizzle

Combining no-churn ice cream, caramel sauce, Dime bars, chocolate sauce and peanut praline, this divine frozen bombe just screams 'EAT ME'! It's best made a day in advance, to give it plenty of time in the freezer. You can also make mini versions in small jelly moulds that total the same volume. As the mix contains raw eggs, it is not suitable for pregnant women, very young children or anyone frail.

SERVES 8–10

12 × 28g Dime bars (in their wrappers)

50g caster sugar

4 eggs, separated

1 tsp vanilla extract

250g mascarpone

400ml double cream

600ml Almond Caramel Sauce (page 182), at room temperature

125ml Chocolate Sauce (page 183), at room temperature

150g peanut Praline (page 183), broken into small shards

ESSENTIAL KIT:

2-litre round, plain-sided bundt tin, jelly mould or bowl

Electric whisk

1. Line the mould with a double layer of cling film, leaving at least 10cm hanging over the edges. With the Dime bars still in their wrappers, smash into small pieces with a rolling pin, then open ten packets and tip into a bowl.

2. Combine the sugar, egg yolks and vanilla extract in a large bowl, and beat in the mascarpone until smooth and well blended.

3. Using an electric whisk, beat the egg whites to stiff peaks. Whisk the cream in a large bowl until just stiff. Fold the cream into the mascarpone mix until blended, then gently fold in the egg whites.

4. Spoon a third of this mix into the mould. Scatter with half the opened Dime bar pieces, placing some close to the outside of the mould, and drizzle with a third of the caramel sauce. Repeat the three layers, finishing with the creamy mix, leaving a third of the caramel sauce for serving. Cover with the excess cling film and freeze for at least 8 hours or overnight until frozen solid.

5. Remove from the freezer 15–20 minutes before serving to soften a little. Unwrap and lay a cake stand or round plate upside down on top. Turn both over together, allowing the bombe to drop down. Remove the mould and peel off the cling film. Drizzle with a few spoonfuls of the caramel sauce and all the chocolate sauce. Scatter with the two reserved packets of Dime bar pieces. Stick half the peanut praline shards into the top and scatter the rest over the top. Serve at once, with the remaining caramel sauce in a small jug.

6. Leftover bombe should be frozen straight away. Freeze individual portions in lidded plastic tubs. They will keep for up to a few months.

Iced Raspberry Crumble-Crunch Sandwiches

Consisting of two crumbly layers of granola sandwiched around a chunk of raspberry ice cream, these are gloriously quick to make – even the ice cream part, which doesn't involve churning. Then you simply layer everything in a tin. Since these will keep in the freezer for a few months, it pays to divide into portions once set, making them easy to grab and go whenever you fancy a frosty little treat. Bear in mind these contain uncooked egg whites, so aren't suitable for pregnant women, very young children or anyone frail.

MAKES 9

Sunflower oil, for greasing

4 egg whites

200g caster sugar

450ml double cream

200g full-fat cream cheese, at room temperature

Juice of 2 lemons

500g fresh raspberries

125ml maple syrup

500g granola, broken up if in clusters

ESSENTIAL KIT:

20cm square, loose-bottomed cake tin, at least 7.5cm deep

Electric whisk

1. Grease the cake tin with oil and line with parchment paper.

2. Using an electric whisk, beat the egg whites and sugar together in a large bowl for 2–3 minutes or until stiff and glossy. Add the cream and continue to whisk for about 2 minutes more until thick and creamy. Finally, add the cream cheese and lemon juice and mix on low until well combined. Lightly crush the raspberries in a small bowl with a fork or masher and gently fold them in with a spatula. Set the mixture aside.

3. Bring the maple syrup to a simmer in a medium saucepan and allow it to bubble away for 1–2 minutes until thickened slightly. Remove from the heat, stir the granola in until evenly coated and spoon half of it into the prepared tin, spreading it evenly all over the base.

4. Pour the creamy raspberry mixture on top, spreading evenly with the back of a spoon. Sprinkle the remaining granola evenly over the top and press it down lightly with your hands. Cover with cling film and freeze for at least 6 hours or overnight until frozen solid.

5. When ready to serve, lift out of the tin, peel off the paper and leave for 10–15 minutes to soften a little. Then, using a long, sharp knife dipped in boiling water and wiped dry before every slice, cut the sandwich into nine even-sized pieces. Serve at once.

6. These portions, wrapped in parchment paper and then cling film to secure, will keep happily in the freezer for a few months, so you can eat one when you please.

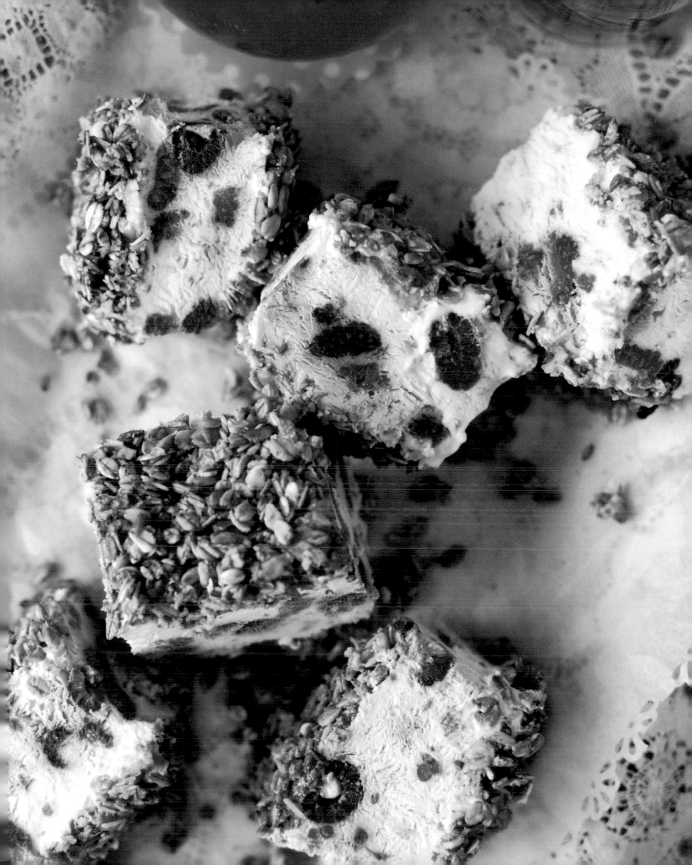

Waffley Good Ice-Cream Sandwiches

These waffle thins can be shaped into cones, cigars or baskets as soon as they come off the panini press: working quickly, wrap them around an appropriate shape and leave to harden. As with pancakes, don't be disheartened if your first try is less than successful – you will get the feel for them in no time. Use a panini-style press (with griddle lines) to get the waffle texture, or a flat sandwich press for thins without the waffle look.

MAKES 10 sandwiches (or 20 waffle thins)

WAFFLE THINS:

250ml double cream

1 tsp vanilla extract

200g plain flour

150g icing sugar

25g cocoa powder

1 tbsp cornflour

⅛ tsp ground cinnamon

Sunflower oil, for greasing

FILLING:

500ml of your choice of ice-cream flavours (pages 184–5 or shop-bought)

2 tbsp in total of your choice of edible sprinkles

ESSENTIAL KIT:

Electric whisk

Panini press

1. First, prepare the waffle thins. Using an electric whisk, beat the cream and vanilla extract in a large bowl until softly whipped. Sift in the flour, icing sugar, cocoa powder, cornflour and cinnamon and mix well to a smooth, soft mixture. Cover with cling film and leave to sit for 20 minutes. Line two large trays with parchment paper.

2. After this time, lightly grease the grill plates of a panini press with some oil on kitchen paper and then turn it on (medium-high if there is an option). When it is ready, spoon in 1 heaped teaspoon of the mixture as a test run. Close the lid and cook for 1–2 minutes until spread and cooked through. Depending on how far the test run spread, you may have room to cook more than one at a time, spaced sufficiently well apart. Spoon in the next batch and cook.

3. Carefully remove using a heatproof spatula and lay on the prepared trays to cool and harden. They are quite fragile so be careful not to break them. Repeat until all the mixture is used, to give 20 in total.

4. Remove the ice cream from the freezer about 5 minutes before serving to soften a little. Scatter the different edible sprinkles on separate plates. When the ice cream is ready, place two small scoops on each of 10 waffle thins and sandwich with another. Dip the exposed ice-cream on both sides into the sprinkles and enjoy straight away.

5. Of course these don't all have to be assembled and eaten at once; the waffle thins keep for up to two weeks in an airtight container.

Snickers Ice-Cream Cake

If you love chocolate, peanuts, caramel and ice cream, this is definitely the cake for you! It is very simple to make, as once you have your sauces and no-churn ice cream prepared, it's just a matter of assembly. Allow enough time for it to freeze properly before serving. If you can't find peanut butter ice cream in the shops, then it really is worth making your own and isn't as tricky as you may think.

SERVES 12–14

250ml Salted Caramel Sauce (page 182)

250ml Chocolate Sauce (page 183)

1.5 litres Peanut Butter Ice Cream (pages 184--5 or shop-bought)

Sunflower oil, for the tin

12 × 58g Snickers bars

15 toffee waffle biscuits

ESSENTIAL KIT:

20cm round, springform cake tin, at least 9cm deep

1. Prepare the caramel sauce and chocolate sauce, if you haven't already. Remove the ice cream from the freezer and leave to soften until spreadable but not completely thawed.

2. Oil the cake tin and line the sides with parchment paper. Cut the Snickers bars into 5mm-thick slices and roughly chop the waffle biscuits into small bite-sized pieces.

3. Scatter a third of the waffle pieces in a single layer in the bottom of the tin. Spoon a third of the ice cream on top and spread evenly. Scatter on a third of the Snickers pieces in a single layer. Drizzle with a third of each of the caramel and chocolate sauces. Repeat these layers again, using the same quantities of everything. Then scatter with the remaining waffle pieces and finish with the remaining ice cream, smoothing the top. You should have a third each of Snickers pieces and caramel and chocolate sauces left for serving. Cover with cling film and freeze for at least 8 hours or overnight until frozen solid.

4. When ready to serve, remove the cake from the tin and sit it on a cake stand or serving plate. Peel off the parchment paper and leave for 15–20 minutes to soften a little. Then, to decorate, arrange the remaining Snickers pieces on top and spoon over the caramel and chocolate sauces so they just dribble down the edges. To serve, cut into 12–14 wedges, which is best done with a long sharp knife, dipped in boiling water and wiped dry between each cut.

5. Leftover ice-cream cake should be frozen straight away. Wrap individual portions in parchment paper and seal in a food bag. These will keep happily in the freezer for up to a few months.

Iced Lemon Meringue Cake

This is really quick and easy as it uses shop-bought meringues and very few other ingredients so there's little preparation. If you're feeling snazzy, turn it into an Alaska by making the meringue topping from page 150 (omitting the peppermint extract), and piping it all over this cake, then blowtorch or grill in the same way.

SERVES 8–10

Sunflower oil, for greasing

1 × 280g shop-bought Madeira cake

450ml double cream

8 shop-bought meringue nests

1 × 320g jar lemon curd

100g flaked almonds

100g crème fraîche

8–10 yellow or orange Crystallised Rose Petals (pages 186–7)

ESSENTIAL KIT:

20cm round, springform cake tin

1. Grease the tin with oil and line the sides with parchment paper. Cut the cake into eight slices, 1.5cm thick, and arrange snugly in the bottom of the tin, breaking into smaller pieces if necessary to fit.

2. Softly whip the cream in a large bowl. Roughly crumble in the meringue nests and fold in gently. Lightly ripple in two-thirds of the lemon curd. Spoon into the tin, spreading evenly. Drizzle with the remaining curd. Cover with cling film and freeze for 8 hours or overnight. This can be prepared up to a few months in advance.

3. Toast the almonds in a dry frying pan on a medium heat, tossing until golden brown. Remove and let cool. Keep airtight until serving.

4. When ready to serve, remove the cake from the tin, place on a stand and peel off the paper. Leave for 5–10 minutes to soften up, then stick the toasted almonds all over the sides. Dollop 8–10 tablespoonfuls (depending on servings) of crème fraîche evenly spaced around the top edge. Place a rose petal on each one. Using a long sharp knife dipped in hot water and wiped dry between slices, cut the cake into 8–10 wedges, each with a dollop of crème fraîche and a petal.

5. Freeze leftovers straight away. Wrap individual portions in parchment paper and seal in a food bag in the freezer for up to a few months.

For an added twist . . .

★ Iced Chocolate Meringue Cake: Line the tin with marbled cake rather than Madeira. Replace the lemon curd with Nutella, warmed a little to loosen. Use chopped toasted hazelnuts instead of almonds and decorate the crème fraîche with chocolate curls.

NO-BAKE
DESSERTS

Sticky Pear & Date Steamed Puds

A slow cooker is a very handy piece of kitchen kit and not just for savoury food. These mini puddings can be safely cooked unattended over a long period of time, making them perfect no-fuss dinnertime treats. If they have been cooked ahead of time (up to 24 hours) they can be warmed through briefly in a microwave. Alternatively, these can be cooked in a steamer for 40 minutes.

MAKES 6

200g pitted dates

1 tsp bicarbonate of soda

250ml boiling water

100g unsalted butter
+ extra for greasing

6 tbsp maple syrup

125g soft light brown sugar

2 eggs

150g self-raising flour

½ tsp ground cinnamon

½ tsp mixed spice

1 large ripe pear

350ml Pecan Caramel Sauce (page 182)

300ml Vanilla Custard (page 186 or shop-bought)

ESSENTIAL KIT:

Slow cooker

6 × 175ml dariole moulds or mini pudding basins

Food processor

1. Set the slow cooker to heat up as per manufacturer's instructions.

2. Place the dates and bicarbonate of soda in a bowl and cover with the boiling water. Leave aside for about 5 minutes while you prepare the moulds.

3. Butter the insides of the moulds or basins really well. Add a tablespoon of maple syrup into the bottom of each and set aside.

4. Drain the dates well and blend them to a smooth purée in a food processor. Add the butter and sugar and blend everything until fairly smooth. Add the eggs, flour, cinnamon and mixed spice and blitz again to combine.

5. Peel, core and finely chop the pear and divide it between the moulds. Ladle the cake mix over, dividing it evenly between them. Sit the puddings into the slow cooker, pop the lid on and leave to slow cook for about 8 hours or until the tip of a knife inserted in the centre of a pudding comes out clean.

6. Make the pecan caramel sauce and custard within the last hour of cooking, if you haven't done so already. Otherwise, simply warm them through on a low heat just before serving.

7. When cooked, remove the puddings from the slow cooker and leave to stand for a couple of minutes. Turn each one out onto the centre of a serving plate to reveal the sticky pear topping. Serve at once with custard and pecan caramel sauce.

Poached Plum Granola Crumble

A classic pudding made with a crunchy granola twist, and turned golden under the grill (unless you consider this cheating, in which case use a blowtorch!). If you don't have a casserole pan suitable to serve at the table then cook the plums in a saucepan and transfer to a baking dish before adding the crumble top. Cinnamon custard is delicious with this: simply add 1 teaspoon of cinnamon instead of the vanilla when making the custard (page 186). It is also delicious served with cream or ice cream.

SERVES 6–8

Finely grated zest and juice of 2 oranges

100g golden caster sugar

1kg ripe plums

Seeds scraped from 1 vanilla pod + the pod

1 star anise

TOPPING.

100ml clear honey

300g granola, broken up if in clusters

600ml Vanilla Custard (page 186 or shop-bought)

ESSENTIAL KIT:

Blowtorch or grill

1. Setting aside the zest for now, measure the orange juice in a jug and make up to 200ml with water if necessary. Pour into a wide shallow casserole pan, sprinkle with the sugar and bring slowly to the boil on a medium heat, stirring until the sugar dissolves. Then allow to boil for two minutes.

2. Meanwhile, halve and de-stone the plums. Add these to the pan, plus the vanilla pod and seeds, orange zest and star anise, reduce the heat and leave to poach gently for 8–10 minutes until softened. Scoop the poached plums out carefully with a slotted spoon and set them aside on a large plate. Turn up the heat and leave the liquid to bubble away for 2–3 minutes until reduced slightly.

3. For the topping, bring the honey to a simmer in a medium pan and allow to bubble for 1–2 minutes until thickened slightly. Remove from the heat and stir in the granola until evenly coated.

4. If using the grill, preheat to medium and set the shelf in the middle. Remove the now-reduced fruity liquid from the heat, carefully fish out the star anise and vanilla pod and discard, and slide the plums back in. Alternatively if you prefer to transfer this to a heatproof serving dish, do so now. Then spoon the granola topping evenly all over. Place under the grill for 1–2 minutes until just catching colour, or brown the top with a blowtorch.

5. Remove and serve at once with the custard.

Black Forest Jam-Jar Gateaux

Jam-jar cakes are fun to make and of course to eat. They can be devoured at home or packed for a picnic, day trip or lunchbox treat. Secure the lid on each jar and decorate with fabric and ribbons if you want to make them look really pretty. Why not come up with your own flavour ideas for different layers every time?

MAKES 4

1 × 400g can pitted cherries in syrup

75g caster sugar

Seeds scraped from 1 vanilla pod

3 tbsp icing sugar

250g mascarpone

100ml double cream

300g shop-bought chocolate brownies (about 2 square portions)

1 tsp cocoa powder

ESSENTIAL KIT:

4 × 250ml jam jars (and lids if necessary)

1. Drain the juice from the can of cherries into a medium frying pan and add the caster sugar and half the vanilla seeds. Bring to a slow boil, stirring until the sugar dissolves, then simmer gently for about 10 minutes until reduced by a quarter and thick and syrupy.

2. Meanwhile, sift the icing sugar into a medium bowl. Add the mascarpone and remaining vanilla seeds, and mix together until smooth and well blended. Softly whip the cream in a separate bowl and fold it into the mixture to loosen it. Cover with cling film and chill in the fridge until ready to assemble. This can be prepared up to 24 hours in advance.

3. Add the cherries to the now reduced syrup and continue to simmer for 1 minute. Remove from the heat and leave to cool completely.

4. When ready to assemble, crumble a 25g piece of brownie into the bottom of each of the four jam jars. Spoon over about a tablespoon of the cooled cherries in syrup and top with a couple of tablespoonfuls of the mascarpone mixture. Repeat the layers twice more until all the ingredients are used up. Dust the tops with cocoa powder through a fine sieve and serve.

For an added twist . . .

★ **Victoria sandwich in a jar:** Layer pieces of shop-bought Madeira cake with Strawberry Purée (page 185) and buttercream icing.

★ **Jam-jar pavlova:** Crumble meringue nests into the jars and layer with Mango Purée (page 185), crushed raspberries and cream that has been softly whipped with vanilla seeds and icing sugar.

Bumblebee Jelly Cake

Okay, so this bumblebee has white stripes instead of black, but you see the resemblance! For the photo, the jelly was set in a sandcastle bucket but you can use any mould you like. With a large mould, the recipe does require quite a few stages to set all the separate layers so it's best to start early in the day, or it can be assembled with fewer layers in small glasses if you need a speedier setting time.

SERVES 8–10

16 gelatine leaves
4 medium mangos
Sunflower oil, for greasing
2 × 400ml cans coconut milk
50g caster sugar
Juice of 1 lime
200ml double cream, to serve

ESSENTIAL KIT:

Food processor
2-litre mould like a (well-cleaned) sandcastle bucket, jelly mould or bundt tin
Wooden skewer or chopstick

1. First, prepare the mango jelly. Soak eight gelatine leaves in a small bowl, with just enough cold water to cover, for 5–10 minutes until soft.

2. Meanwhile, peel and chop the mango and blend the flesh in a food processor for a minute or two until really smooth. Pour about a quarter of this into a medium saucepan and warm through on a gentle heat, removing just as it comes to the boil. Squeezing the excess water off, stir the now-softened gelatine into the warm mango until dissolved. Pour this back into the remaining mango purée and measure it in a jug: there should be 925ml of purée in total. If there's less, simply make it up with water. Leave to cool completely.

3. Lightly oil the inside of your mould and set aside. Using a sharp knife, make a score mark on a wooden skewer or chopstick at 1.5cm from the non-pointed end of the stick. This will be used to ensure even-sized layers as you build up the jelly.

4. Once the mango jelly is cool, stand the stick, non-pointed side down, on the base of the mould. Pour enough jelly mixture in to reach the score mark and remove the stick. Cover the mould with cling film and chill in the fridge for 45–60 minutes until set firm. Put aside the remaining jelly for now, covered but out of the fridge.

5. Meanwhile, prepare the coconut jelly. Soak the remaining gelatine as before. Pour one can of coconut milk into a small saucepan, add the sugar and cook over a gentle heat, stirring until the

CONTINUED ⇒

▨ *CONTINUED FROM OVERLEAF*

sugar dissolves. Remove from the heat and stir in the lime juice. Squeezing the excess water off, stir the now-softened gelatine into the mixture, until dissolved. Pour into a large measuring jug, stir in the remaining can of coconut milk and leave to cool completely. There should also be 925ml, so both jellies are equal.

6. Once the first layer of mango jelly is set, rest the non-pointed end of the stick gently on it (being careful not to pierce it) and pour in enough coconut jelly to reach the score mark, then remove the stick. Again, cover and chill the jelly in the mould for the same time until set. Put aside the remaining jelly, out of the fridge.

7. Repeat this process, alternating the mango and coconut layers, until both mixtures have been used up. You should have five layers of each, ending with the coconut jelly. If either mixture begins to set in the jug as you go, very gently warm it through (on the hob or in the microwave) for the minimum time possible until it is liquidy again. Be careful not to pour this onto the set jelly in the mould until it has completely cooled again or you will melt the set jelly.

8. Once the final layer has been added, give the jelly a good 3 hours in the fridge to set really firmly. When ready to serve, remove the jelly from the mould by gently pulling it away with your fingers all around the edge of the mould, to release the air lock. Place a cake stand or serving plate upside down on top of the mould, turn it over carefully and give it a gentle shake to help it wiggle out and onto the plate. Cut the jelly into four or five wedges, lay each piece flat and then halve them across to give 8–10 portions in total. This is delicious served with a little cream poured over the top.

Individual Autumn Puddings

Inspired by classic summer pudding but adapted for a different season, these little puddings have a brioche bread case and rich fruity filling. You can use slices of white bread instead of brioche if you prefer. Alternatively, make one large pudding using a 1.5-litre basin.

SERVES 6

375g fresh blackberries

125g soft light brown sugar

125ml red wine

4 tbsp crème de cassis (or blackcurrant cordial)

400g ripe plums, de-stoned and roughly chopped

400g Bramley apples, peeled, cored and roughly chopped

1 slightly stale brioche loaf, cut into about 20 × 1cm slices

6 small mint sprigs

200ml crème fraîche

ESSENTIAL KIT:

6 × 175ml dariole moulds or mini pudding basins

Food processor

6cm and 7.5cm round straight-sided cutters

1. Line the moulds with cling film, leaving 5cm excess, and set on a tray. Blitz about a third of the blackberries in a food processor until smooth and pour into a large saucepan. Add the sugar, red wine and crème de cassis or cordial, and bring to a simmer on a medium heat.

2. Stir the chopped plums and apples into the sauce, along with the remaining blackberries. Simmer for 10–15 minutes, stirring occasionally until the apple is soft. Remove from the heat and leave to cool.

3. With the smaller cutter, stamp out six circles from six slices of brioche. Pop one into the base of each mould to fit snugly. With the larger cutter, stamp out another six circles and set aside for the tops. Remove the crusts from the remaining brioche slices and cut into quarters. Line the inside of each mould with about five pieces, standing upright and overlapping slightly, trimming if necessary.

4. Drain the fruit mixture through a colander over a bowl, reserving the liquid in the fridge for serving. Spoon the fruit into the brioche-lined moulds, packing it in firmly and filling almost to the top. Press a brioche lid on each mould and cover with the excess cling film. Sit a heavy tray on top of the moulds and wrap cling film around the whole thing so it presses down tightly and helps firm up the puddings. Chill for at least 3 hours or overnight, until firm.

5. To serve, lift the puddings out of their moulds by the cling film. Turn each one over onto the centre of a serving plate and remove the cling film. Using a brush, dab the reserved fruit sauce all over the outside, especially on any white patches. Spoon over the remaining sauce, garnish with mint and serve with crème fraîche.

Raspberry & Custard Trifle Bowl Cake

This gorgeous cakey twist on a trifle contains all those classic ingredients presented in a totally different way! It can be made a day or two in advance, which is helpful as it does involve a few stages.

SERVES 10–12

12 gelatine leaves

500g frozen raspberries

75g caster sugar

3 × 185g shop-bought jam Swiss rolls

3 tbsp sherry, optional

125g fresh raspberries

600ml Vanilla Custard (page 186 or shop-bought)

200ml double cream

ESSENTIAL KIT:

From a set of bowls that nestle inside each other:

2.5-litre bowl (roughly 23cm across the top, 13cm deep)

1.5-litre bowl (roughly 16cm across the top, 9cm deep)

1. Soak seven gelatine leaves in just enough cold water to cover, for 5–10 minutes until soft. Warm the frozen raspberries, sugar and 400ml of water in a medium pan on a gentle heat for 5 minutes, stirring until the sugar dissolves. Pour into a fine sieve over a bowl and push through. Squeezing out excess water, stir the soft gelatine into the raspberry liquid, until dissolved. Leave to cool.

2. Line the larger bowl with a double layer of cling film, leaving 10cm hanging over the rim. Cut the Swiss rolls into 2cm-thick slices and line the bowl in a single layer, packing them tightly to avoid gaps. Save about six slices. If using, dab sherry all over with a brush.

3. Line the smaller bowl with double cling film as before. Pour in the cooled raspberry mix and stir in the fresh raspberries. Cover with the excess cling film and chill for at least 3 hours until set.

4. Soak the remaining gelatine as before, until soft. Make the custard if you haven't yet, or reheat it gently. Squeezing out excess water, stir the soft gelatine into the custard, until dissolved. Leave to cool completely.

5. To assemble, lift out the jelly, quickly turn it over on the palm of your hand, peel off the cling film and flip it back into the cake-lined bowl. Pour the cool custard on top. Cover and chill. After 1 hour, lay the remaining cake slices over the custard, replace the cling film and return to the fridge for 2 hours until set.

6. To serve, lightly whip the cream and spoon into a serving bowl. Open up the cling film and place a serving plate or cake stand upside down on the bowl. Turn the whole thing over, and lift off the bowl and cling film to reveal the trifle cake.

Irish Crème Brûlée Cups with Hazelnut Praline

These impressive no-bake brûlées make for a handy, stress-free dinner party dessert as they can be made 24 hours in advance. You can set the brûlée mixture in shop-bought chocolate cups or 125ml ramekins, pretty glasses or tea cups for a speedier pud. The waffle thins in the Waffley Good Ice-Cream Sandwiches (page 157) make a good substitute for the praline if you prefer.

MAKES 10

CRÈME BRÛLÉE:

2 gelatine leaves

300ml Irish cream liqueur

250ml double cream

250ml whole milk

8 large egg yolks

75g caster sugar

2 tbsp cornflour

1 tsp vanilla extract

CHOCOLATE CUPS:

400g dark chocolate (at least 70% cocoa solids)

TO DECORATE:

250g Hazelnut Praline (page 183)

1 tsp cocoa powder

ESSENTIAL KIT:

12-hole muffin tin

10 paper muffin cases

1. Soak the gelatine leaves in a small bowl, with just enough cold water to cover, for 5–10 minutes until soft.

2. Pour the cream liqueur, cream and milk into a large, wide saucepan and slowly bring to the boil over a medium heat. Meanwhile, beat the egg yolks, sugar, cornflour and vanilla extract together in a large jug until smooth and well blended. Remove the cream mixture from the heat as soon as it comes to the boil and gradually pour it into the egg mixture, stirring all the time. Return the whole lot to the saucepan and bring to a gentle simmer over a low heat, stirring constantly until thickened enough to coat the back of the spoon.

3. Remove from the heat. Squeeze the excess water from the now-softened gelatine and stir into the mixture until dissolved. Pop a piece of cling film directly on the surface to prevent a skin from forming and leave to cool completely.

4. To make the chocolate cups: line the muffin tin with the cases. Snap the chocolate into a medium heatproof bowl and melt either in the microwave in 30-second blasts, stirring between each go, or over a pan of simmering water, shallow enough that the water doesn't touch the bowl. When melted, stir and remove from the heat.

5. Spoon a tablespoon of melted chocolate into a paper case and use a small brush to spread it from the bottom up the insides to coat completely. Repeat with the other nine cases. About three-quarters of the chocolate should remain so set this aside for now. Pop the muffin tin in the freezer for 20 minutes, until the cups are set.

CONTINUED

CONTINUED FROM OVERLEAF

6. Repeat the process of coating with chocolate and freezing to set three more times, to give four layers in total. The melted chocolate will cool to room temperature, which is perfect for adding layers without melting the previous layer (if you work quickly), but it should not be allowed to set. If it does, then melt it again as before, but very briefly not letting it become too warm.

7. Once the four layers are complete and set, and with cool hands, carefully peel the paper cases away from the chocolate to reveal the fluted cups. Arrange them on a tray lined with parchment paper as you go.

8. Divide the now-cooled filling evenly between the chocolate cups, levelling the tops. Chill in the fridge for at least 4 hours until completely set. These can be made up to a day in advance.

9. If you haven't already made the hazelnut praline, now is a good time to do so. When ready to serve, dust the crème brûlée filling with cocoa powder through a fine sieve. Break the praline into ten chunks and stick one upright in the top of each cup. Serve on a pretty little plate.

White Chocolate
& Pistachio Tiramisu

A white chocolate version of the classic tiramisu, this can be put together fairly quickly ahead of time, then popped in the fridge to let the flavours develop at their leisure. Chopped pistachios and white chocolate curls give an attractive finish. Marsala is an Italian fortified wine that is often used in cooking, or you can use Vin Santo (a dessert wine), sherry or a coffee liqueur like Tia Maria or Kahlúa.

SERVES 6

SPONGE LAYER:

500ml strong coffee

75g caster sugar

75ml Marsala (see intro, above)

200g sponge fingers

CREAMY LAYER:

100g white chocolate

225ml double cream

250g mascarpone

50g icing sugar

Seeds scraped from 1 vanilla pod

TO DECORATE:

Large handful of white Chocolate Curls (page 184)

50g shelled green pistachios, roughly chopped

ESSENTIAL KIT:

25cm × 18cm baking or serving dish, at least 10cm deep and 1.7 litres in volume

1. Pour the coffee and sugar into a wide saucepan and bring to the boil, stirring until the sugar dissolves. Leave to bubble away for 2–3 minutes until reduced by half, then remove from the heat.

2. Snap the white chocolate for the creamy layer into a small heatproof bowl, add 50ml of cream and melt in the microwave in 30-second blasts, stirring between each go, or over a pan of simmering water, shallow enough that the water doesn't touch the bowl. When melted, stir until smooth and leave to cool to body temperature.

3. Add the Marsala to the coffee mixture and pour into a wide dish. Place half the sponge fingers in the liquid to soak for up to 1 minute, turning once, until just soft (but not soggy and breaking). Arrange in neat rows in the bottom of the serving dish. Set aside the remaining coffee liquid for later.

4. Back to the creamy layer: beat the mascarpone in a large bowl for a minute to loosen. Sift in the icing sugar and beat in along with the vanilla seeds. Whisk the remaining 175ml of cream in another bowl until just stiff. Beat the cooled chocolate into the mascarpone, then fold in the whipped cream. Spoon half of this on top of the sponge fingers and spread out evenly. Soak the remaining sponge fingers in the remaining coffee liquid as before and arrange on top. Spread with the remaining mascarpone mixture. Cover with cling film and chill for at least 3 hours until firm. This can be prepared up to 24 hours in advance.

5. If you haven't yet done so, make the white chocolate curls. To serve, scatter chopped pistachios on top and decorate with chocolate curls.

Chilled Orange Soufflés with Pistachio Crusts

This is a classic cold soufflé recipe but the mix is set above the teacup rims so it looks risen like a hot soufflé. Parchment paper helps achieve the 'rise', so it's worth taking the time to ensure it is attached securely. As this is made using uncooked egg whites, it isn't suitable for very young children, pregnant women or anyone frail.

SERVES 6

4 gelatine leaves

4 large eggs, separated

125g caster sugar

Finely grated zest and juice of 3 oranges

150ml double cream

25g shelled green pistachios, roughly chopped

ESSENTIAL KIT:

6 × 125ml teacups or ramekins

A pair of helping hands at the beginning or a paperclip

String

Electric whisk

1. Wrap a strip of parchment around the outside of each teacup or ramekin, ensuring the paper is at least 2.5cm taller, and hold it in place with a paperclip or pair of helping hands, while you secure it with string. Arrange on a tray and set aside.

2. Soak the gelatine leaves in a small bowl, with just enough cold water to cover, for 5–10 minutes until soft.

3. Place the egg yolks, sugar and orange zest in a large heatproof bowl over a pan of simmering water. Beat with an electric whisk for 10 minutes until thick and creamy. Remove from the heat, press cling film directly on the surface to prevent a skin forming, and let cool.

4. Warm a third of the orange juice in a small saucepan on the hob or bowl in the microwave until simmering, then remove from the heat. Squeezing off excess water, drop in the soft gelatine, stirring until dissolved. Add the remaining orange juice and leave to cool.

5. Whisk the egg whites to soft peaks: when you lift a bit of egg white on the whisk, the peak should droop slightly. In another bowl, whisk the cream until just stiff.

6. Stir the orange juice mix into the egg yolk mixture. Gently fold in the whites until well blended, followed by the cream. Spoon into the teacups to sit just above the tops, levelling the surface with the back of a spoon. Chill for at least 3 hours or overnight until set.

7. To serve, carefully peel off the paper, using the tip of a small sharp knife if necessary. Stick the pistachios against the now-exposed soufflé edge and serve.

Eat-The-Bowl Peanut Butter Puds

These homemade chocolate bowls are filled with scrumptious cake, peanut butter whip and strawberry purée, but you can fill them with anything you like from fruit to ice cream. Water-based food colouring will probably cause melted chocolate to seize and go grainy. However, there is a product called Flo-Coat by AmeriColor (available in all good baking stores or online) that will allow you to use water-based colouring successfully to dye the chocolate. Alternatively, simply use oil-based or powdered food colouring.

SERVES 6

CUPS:

100g white chocolate

Oil-based or powdered food colouring(s)

OR

Water-based food colouring(s) + AmeriColor Flo-Coat (see intro)

PEANUT BUTTER WHIP:

125g smooth peanut butter

75g full-fat cream cheese, at room temperature

25g icing sugar

75ml double cream

TO SERVE:

200g Strawberry Purée (page 185)

100g shop-bought marbled Madeira cake, cut into bite-sized cubes

6 large fresh strawberries, roughly chopped

1 tbsp edible sprinkles

ESSENTIAL KIT OVERLEAF ➡

1. First, the really fun bit: making the cups. Snap the chocolate into a medium heatproof bowl and melt either in the microwave in 30-second blasts, stirring between each go, or over a pan of simmering water, shallow enough that the water doesn't touch the bowl. When melted, give it a stir and remove from the heat.

2. At this stage you can either add one food colouring to the whole amount or divide it up into two or three equal batches and add different colours to each one (blue, pink and green were used for the photo). Alternatively, just leave the chocolate as it is to make white cups. Add the food colouring 1 drop at a time, stirring between each addition, until you reach your preferred shade. If using water-based colour, add 6 drops of AmeriColor Flo-Coat first, before every 1 drop of colour. Avoid adding too much colour as it may give the chocolate a bitter taste. Leave to cool for about 5 minutes as the hot chocolate may burst the balloons.

3. Meanwhile, line a large baking sheet with parchment paper. Blow up six balloons, tie them closed, wash and dry them and set aside. It is wise to prepare a few extras in case any burst without warning!

4. When cooled, dip the bottom of a balloon into the melted chocolate, rolling it around if necessary so that it comes about 5cm up the sides. The top of the chocolate cup can be straight or wavy depending on how you decide to dip and roll it. Allow the excess to

CONTINUED ➡

⟹ CONTINUED FROM OVERLEAF

ESSENTIAL KIT:

6 water bomb balloons + some extras in case of explosions!

Regular or disposable piping bag, fitted with a star nozzle

drip off and then sit it upright on the lined tray while you repeat with the remaining balloons. A little pool of chocolate may gather at the bottom of each balloon cup on the tray, but this is perfect as a stand for the cup later. Chill in the fridge for at least 30 minutes until set hard. These can be made up to a few days in advance.

5. Meanwhile, make the peanut butter filling. Beat the peanut butter and cream cheese in a large bowl until well blended. Sift in the icing sugar and beat to combine. Softly whip the cream in another bowl and fold it into the peanut butter until well mixed. Spoon the mixture into the prepared piping bag and set aside in the fridge until ready to use. This can be made a day in advance.

6. Once the chocolate cups are set, remove from the fridge, snip the tied end of the balloon with scissors to let the air out, and carefully peel the balloon out from the chocolate cup. This can be done as soon as the cups are set, to free up some fridge space after the balloon takeover! If you haven't already, make the strawberry purée.

7. When ready to assemble, sit the chocolate cups on a tray or serving plates. Divide the Madeira squares evenly between the cups and scatter with strawberries. Gently massage the peanut butter whip in the piping bag briefly to loosen it up a little and then pipe a whippy peak on top. Drizzle a little strawberry purée on top and serve the rest in a small jug. Finally, scatter with edible sprinkles and serve.

Raspberry Croissant Custard Pudding

With fresh raspberries, warm custard and buttery croissants, this is a divinely comforting twist on a bread and butter pudding but without the need for an oven. Grilling the pudding caramelises the top, giving it a glossy, freshly baked look that will fool anyone, or if you consider this cheating, use a blowtorch instead. Try making this with brioche, panettone slices or plain bread instead of croissants.

SERVES 6–8

6 croissants

75g unsalted butter, softened

75g apricot jam

125g fresh raspberries

400ml double cream

400ml whole milk

8 large egg yolks

75g caster sugar

2 tbsp cornflour

Seeds scraped from 1 vanilla pod

3 tbsp icing sugar

ESSENTIAL KIT:

23cm square baking dish, at least 6cm deep and 2 litres in volume

Blowtorch or grill

1. Halve the croissants horizontally and spread the butter over the cut sides, followed by the apricot jam. Arrange the croissant halves with the pretty side of the top half and the cut side of the bottom half facing upwards, in a slightly overlapping layer, in the baking dish. With the back of a fork, lightly crush the raspberries in a small bowl and spoon into the gaps around the croissants. Set aside.

2. Prepare the custard. Pour the cream and milk into a large saucepan and slowly bring to the boil over a medium heat. Meanwhile, beat the egg yolks, sugar, cornflour and vanilla seeds together in a large jug, until smooth and well blended. As soon as the cream mixture comes to the boil, remove from the heat and gradually pour it into the egg mixture, stirring constantly. Return the whole mixture to the pan and bring to a gentle simmer over a medium heat, stirring all the time. While continuing to stir constantly, allow it to bubble for 6–8 minutes until thick enough to coat the back of the spoon.

3. Remove from the heat, and gradually pour the custard over the croissants, allowing it to sink down between them before adding more. At this stage, it might not look like the most attractive thing but don't worry, we're not finished with it yet!

4. Once all the custard is added, cover with foil to keep warm and leave to steep for about 10 minutes. If using the grill, set to a medium heat with the shelf in the middle. Dust the pudding liberally with icing sugar through a fine sieve. Then pop under the grill for 2–3 minutes until the top has a nice, rich golden-brown glaze. See, much prettier! Alternatively, use a blowtorch. Serve at once.

PANTRY

Heavenly Caramel Sauce

Just lick this from a spoon (once cool enough!) to find out exactly why it's called heavenly. But be warned: it's so moreish you might have to make double the quantity if you also plan to use it in an actual recipe, such as Build Your Own S'Mores (page 23)!

MAKES 250ml

75g caster sugar ★ 75g soft light brown sugar ★ 75g unsalted butter ★ 75ml double cream

1. Place the caster sugar in a large, heavy-based, stainless-steel (so you can see the colour) saucepan with 3 tablespoons of water and bring to the boil over a medium heat, stirring occasionally.

2. Reduce the heat and simmer, without stirring, for 6–8 minutes until amber in colour. Remove from the heat and add the brown sugar, butter and cream. The mixture will bubble, spit and become lumpy but just stir vigorously until it dies down.

3. Return to the heat, turn it up and allow to bubble for a further 2 minutes, continuing to stir until it forms a smooth thick sauce. Remove from the heat and serve either warm or at room temperature. Once cool, this will keep for 2–3 days in an airtight container in the fridge.

Salted Caramel Sauce

Sweet and salty together is a divine combination. Why not add chocolate to the mix as well, by using this in the Turtleback Terrine (page 30) or the Snickers Ice-Cream Cake (page 158).

MAKES 250ml

As above, but add 1½ teaspoons of fine sea salt along with the cream.

Nutty Caramel Sauce

This nutty version of the heavenly sauce works wonders in the Dime Bar Bombe (page 153), Sticky Pear & Date Steamed Puds (page 162) or Banana & Toffee Waffle Freezer Cake (page 149).

MAKES 300ml

As main sauce recipe, but add 50g of toasted and roughly chopped almonds or pecans along with the cream.

Caramelised Nuts

Caramelising nuts might sound a little scary but it is actually very easy. Serve them scattered over cakes and ice creams or as a delicious snack, or they go surprisingly well with cheese. Try them in Sweet Cinnamon & Ricotta Tortilla Triangles (page 136) or Upside-Down Banana 'Pan' Cakes (page 49).

MAKES 150g

Seeds scraped from 1 vanilla pod + the pod ★ 75g caster sugar ★ 100g nuts, like whole almonds, pecans, hazelnuts, macadamias or walnuts (either separately or mixed)

1. Line a large baking tray with parchment paper or a non-stick cooking mat and set aside.

2. Add the vanilla seeds and pod, the sugar and 3 tablespoons of cold water to a medium, heavy-based, stainless-steel saucepan. Bring to a simmer on a medium heat, without stirring. Bubble for 4–5 minutes until a rich amber colour, again not stirring. Carefully fish out the vanilla pod with tongs, then stir in the nuts quickly to coat.

3. Working fast before they set, tip out onto the prepared tray, spread evenly and leave to harden and cool completely. Once set, break the nuts apart. Store for up to two weeks in an airtight container.

Praline

Praline is basically a nutty sugar caramel set to a firm shard. When broken, bashed or blitzed it can be scattered over desserts, folded through ice cream or stuck onto a cake as decoration. Try it in the Cookie Monster Ice Box Cake (page 52), Raspberry & Chocolate Crepeathon Cake (page 42) or Irish Crème Brûlée Cups (page 173).

MAKES 525g

100g nuts, like salted peanuts, whole almonds, pecans, hazelnuts, macadamias or walnuts (either separately or mixed) ★ 450g caster sugar

1. Line a large baking tray with parchment paper or a non-stick cooking mat and set aside.

2. Roughly chop the nuts or leave whole (depending on size or preference), and toast in a medium, dry frying pan over a gentle heat until golden and fragrant. Remove from the heat and set aside.

3. Put the sugar into a small, heavy-based, stainless-steel saucepan with 125ml of water and bring slowly to the boil on a medium heat, stirring until the sugar dissolves. Allow to bubble for 6–8 minutes, not stirring, until it turns a rich, dark, golden colour.

4. Immediately remove from the heat, stir in the nuts to coat and tip out onto the prepared tray. It will spread but give it a bit of help if necessary by tilting the tray. The mixture will be incredibly hot so be careful not to touch it. Leave to harden and cool completely for about 15 minutes.

5. Once set, break the shard apart into smaller pieces with your hands or bash with a rolling pin. Alternatively, break into pieces and blitz to rough crumbs in a food processor. Either way, the pieces will keep for up to a week in an airtight container. Shards should be layered between parchment paper, while crumbs will be fine in a pile but will need to be broken apart on serving.

Chocolate Sauce

Chocolate sauce is easy to make and so rewarding! Use in the Banana Split Sundae Kamikaze Cake (page 139), Dime Bar Bombe (page 153), Snickers Ice-Cream Cake (page 158) or Build Your Own S'Mores (page 23).

MAKES 500ml

200g dark (at least 70% cocoa solids) or milk chocolate ★ 200ml double cream ★ 100ml whole milk ★ 1 tbsp unsalted butter

1. Snap the chocolate into a large heatproof bowl and melt either in the microwave in 30-second blasts, stirring between each go, or over a pan of simmering water, shallow enough that the water doesn't touch the bowl. When melted, remove from the heat and set aside.

2. Put the cream, milk and butter into a medium pan and bring to a simmer over a medium heat. Once simmering, remove and pour into the melted chocolate, stirring all the time until evenly blended to a smooth chocolate sauce.

3. This can be made in advance and stored for 2–3 days in the fridge. Warm through gently in 30-second blasts in the microwave or over a pan of simmering water, until pourable.

Chocolate Ganache

Chocolate ganache is an even richer version of the chocolate sauce in that it doesn't contain milk. Because of this, it is beautifully thick and sets firm, so is perfect for spreading and coating. If you need an excuse to make it, try Minty Chocolate Fudge Bars (page 60), Upside-Down & Inside-Out Peanut Butter Cheesecake Bombe (page 90) or Death by Chocolate & Blackberry Cheesecake (page 95).

MAKES 400ml

As Chocolate Sauce recipe above, but omit the milk.

Chocolate Curls

It can take a bit of playing around to find the right chocolate temperature for the perfect curls, but once you get the hang of it you will be chuffed at your amazing curled creations. If you have leftover chocolate pieces that are too small to shave from – besides simply gobbling them up, you can finely grate over desserts or use in chocolate sauce or ganache (page 183). Show off your curls in Deep-Pan Double Chocolate Mousse Pie (page 109), Frozen Mocha Chocca Cups (page 144) or White Chocolate & Pistachio Tiramisu (page 175).

MAKES a few handfuls, enough to decorate 1 cake

100g bar of white, milk or dark chocolate

ESSENTIAL KIT: Microwave

1. Line a small, deep tray with parchment paper and set aside.

2. Unwrap and place the chocolate bar on a plate and microwave on high for 5-second intervals, until slightly softened but not hot or melted. The white chocolate will need less time than the milk or dark chocolate. If it becomes too soft then chill in the fridge or freezer briefly to reset.

3. Using a long, sharp knife and starting at one long edge (for wide curls) or a short edge (for narrower curls), drag the knife carefully towards you across the chocolate to shave off curls. If the shavings crumble and crack, the chocolate is not soft enough and so needs to be warmed a little more in the microwave.

4. Carefully slide the curls into the prepared tray and when all are complete, either use straight away or cover with cling film and store for up to a week in the fridge.

Quick & Easy No-Churn Ice Cream

This simple, no-fuss ice cream requires no ice-cream machine, no churning and no stirring. Just freeze until set. There really is no reason not to make it (in every flavour!). Why not freeze individual portions in lidded containers or even cupcake cases set in a muffin tray. Try vanilla in Retro & Soul Arctic Roll (page 141), coffee in Frozen Mocha Chocca Cups (page 144), mint in Minty Fresh Alaska Iceberg (page 150) or the Watermelon Bombe (page 147), and peanut butter in the Snickers Ice-Cream Cake (page 158). Or go for a hat-trick, with raspberry, chocolate and vanilla in the Banana Split Sundae Kamikaze Cake (page 139)!

Basic Recipe

1 × 400ml can condensed milk ★ 500ml double cream

ESSENTIAL KIT: Electric whisk

Mix the condensed milk and additions required for your choice of flavour (see below right) in a large bowl until thick and stiff. Using an electric whisk, beat the cream in a separate bowl, until stiff also. Fold the cream into the condensed milk mixture until well blended. Spoon into a lidded plastic or foil container and freeze for at least 6 hours or overnight until solid. This will keep for up to three months in the freezer. Remove 10–20 minutes before serving (depending on size of block and how warm your room is) until soft enough to scoop.

Vanilla:

MAKES 800ml

Seeds from 1 vanilla pod or 2 tsp vanilla extract

Mint:

MAKES 800ml

½ tsp peppermint extract ★ Few drops of green food colouring, as you wish ★ Optional: 100g roughly chopped dark or milk chocolate, for mint choc chip ice cream

Coffee:

MAKES 850ml

2 tbsp instant espresso coffee powder ★ Optional: 2 tbsp coffee liqueur (like Kahlúa or Tia Maria)

Chocolate:

MAKES 900ml

100g dark chocolate (at least 70% cocoa solids), melted and left to come to body temperature before adding into the mix

Peanut butter:

MAKES 950ml

150g smooth or crunchy peanut butter ★ Optional: you can also try rippling through some strawberry jam

Raspberry, Strawberry or Mixed Berry:

MAKES 975ml

175g Berry Purée (see right)

Fruit Purée

Fruit purées are usually served cold, drizzled over desserts, or rippled through ice cream or natural yoghurt. They can be frozen in ice cube trays for ease of use. Add booze for a grown-up version – peach schnapps is great with mango purée and crème de cassis with any of the berry ones. Purées feature in many recipes in this book, including Strawberry Charlotte (page 36), Mango & Passionfruit Muffin Cup Cheesecakes (page 83), Candy-Stripe Blueberry Cheesecake (page 93) and Blackberry Swirl Marshmallow Gateau (page 27).

ESSENTIAL KIT: Food processor or liquidiser

Raspberry or Strawberry Purée:

MAKES 175g (raspberry) or 200g (strawberry)

250g fresh raspberries or 250g fresh strawberries ★ Optional: 1–3 tsp icing sugar ★ Optional: a little lime juice

Wash the berries and remove any green tops. Blend in a food processor or liquidiser until completely smooth. Pass through a sieve into a bowl. If you like, add sifted icing sugar a teaspoon at a time to give your preferred sweetness or add a squeeze of lime juice for a bit of bite. This is ready to serve but will keep for 2–3 days, covered in the fridge.

Blueberry or Blackberry Purée:

MAKES 125g

125g fresh blueberries or blackberries

Rinse the berries and simmer in a medium saucepan on a gentle heat with a small dash of water for 4–5 minutes until softened, tossing occasionally. Blend in a food processor or liquidiser until really smooth. This will keep for 2–3 days, covered in the fridge.

Mango Purée:

MAKES 150g

1 medium mango

To prepare the mango, slice the cheeks off on each side of the stone. Cut each cheek in half lengthways and peel by running your knife under the flesh close to the skin. Remove the remaining thin strips of mango from each side of the stone and peel in the same way. Roughly chop all the flesh and blitz in a food processor or liquidiser until completely smooth. This will keep for 2–3 days, covered in the fridge.

Peach, Nectarine or Apricot Purée:

MAKES 225g (peach or nectarine) or 175g (apricot)

2 medium peaches or nectarines (about 300g) or 6 apricots (about 250g)

Quarter and de-stone the fruit, and roughly chop the flesh. Blend in a food processor or liquidiser until completely smooth. Pass through a sieve into a bowl. This is best used straight away as it discolours quickly.

Vanilla custard

You really can't beat homemade custard! It is fairly simple to make, and mostly involves standing around stirring, during which time you can daydream about your favourite no-bake bakes. It's important to stir constantly to avoid the egg cooking into lumps. If you are unfortunate enough for this to happen then be sure to pass the custard through a sieve. Homemade custard is slightly thinner than its shop-bought counterpart but you will love how wonderfully smooth and silky it is. Use in Raspberry & Custard Trifle Bowl Cake (page 170), or to accompany the Sticky Pear & Date Steamed Puds (page 162) or Poached Plum Granola Crumble (page 163).

MAKES 600ml

250ml whole milk ★ 250ml double cream ★ Seeds scraped from 1 vanilla pod + the pod ★ 5 egg yolks ★ 100g golden caster sugar ★ 2 tsp cornflour

1. Place the milk, cream and vanilla pod and seeds in a medium saucepan and slowly bring to the boil. When it reaches boiling point, immediately remove from the heat and set aside.

2. Beat the egg yolks, sugar and cornflour together in a large bowl until smooth. Remove the vanilla pod from the milk mixture and pour the milk into the egg mixture, stirring all the time. Pour everything back into the pan and return to a medium heat. While stirring continuously, allow the custard to simmer for 6–8 minutes until thickened enough to coat the back of a spoon.

3. Pass through a fine sieve into a warm jug to serve. If making ahead of time, press cling film down all over the actual surface of the custard (to prevent a skin forming) and leave to cool completely. When required, warm it through on a low heat, stirring constantly, and without allowing it to boil.

Crystallised Rose Petals

You can crystallise just about anything, from edible flowers to fruits and herbs. It is especially fun to do at Christmas time, with bunches of grapes, cranberries, plums, cinnamon sticks, rosemary stalks and holly leaves. Arrange them in a beautiful display or as place settings and watch them sparkle in the twinkly light. These petals shouldn't be attempted on a humid day as the moisture will cause the sugar to clump. Arrange them decoratively on cakes and desserts. And yes, they really can be eaten! Use in Rosewater & Lemon Krispie Roll (page 50), Coconut & Almond Pashka (page 84) or Iced Lemon Meringue Cake (page 160).

MAKES 20–30

20–30 petals from unsprayed (organically grown) rose(s) ★ 1 egg white ★ 100g caster sugar

1. Make sure the rose petals are clean and dry. Lightly beat the egg white in a small bowl and tip the sugar into another.

2. One by one, brush the egg white onto the rose petals with a small brush. Immediately dip each one in the sugar to coat, sprinkling it over by hand where necessary. Another small brush will help to coat them evenly and remove any clumps.

3. Arrange on a cooling rack as you go and leave to dry for at least 2 hours, but about 12 hours for them to become really crisp if you can.

4. The petals will be hard and brittle once well dried out so handle carefully. These can be stored for up to two months in an airtight container.

working quickly and carefully, pour the mixture into the prepared tin. Don't be tempted to touch as it will be incredibly hot. Swirl the tin (but be careful as the bottom will be really hot too) to spread it evenly and then leave until completely cool and set hard.

4. Lift out of the tin, snap into pieces and nibble away. Any surviving honeycomb can be stored for 2–3 days, layered between parchment paper in an airtight container.

Honeycomb

Honeycomb makes an excellent topping for all sorts of sweet goodies, such as Banoffee Cornflake Crust Pie (page 115). Stick shards in the top of any dessert, crumble into ice cream or blitz to rough crumbs in a food processor and sprinkle over cakes. You can buy glucose in most supermarkets or try a good baking supply store. The honeycomb pieces are also delicious coated in chocolate.

MAKES 225g

Sunflower oil, for greasing ★ 175g caster sugar ★ 75g glucose syrup ★ ½ tsp bicarbonate of soda

ESSENTIAL KIT: 18cm fixed-based cake tin

1. Line the tin with parchment paper, lightly oiled on both sides, and set aside.

2. Place the sugar and glucose syrup in a medium, stainless-steel saucepan with 50ml of water and bring to the boil on a high heat, stirring until the sugar dissolves. Then, without stirring, allow to bubble for 5–6 minutes until it turns a good golden honeycomb colour.

3. Add the bicarbonate of soda – it will bubble and froth but just stir it in for a few seconds. Then,

INDEX

THANKS

To the big dream team who helped make my first cookbook a fabulous reality, here's wishing you all the no-bake bakes your hearts desire.

The biggest wedge of cake goes to the cookbook queens from Quercus towers, Jenny Heller and Ione Walder. Super-hero Jenny saved me late one night with the wise words 'stressed is actually desserts spelled backwards'. I am in awe of Ione's special magic powers, which include excessive word culling and the ability to keep everything running smoothly in a girl-next-door kind of way. You have both made my sweet dreams come true, for which I am eternally grateful. Thanks for having faith in me to not burn all the buns!

More cake slices to the rest of team Quercus, including copy editor Sarah Chatwin, designers Nicky Barneby, Nick Clark, Paul Oakley and David Eldridge, and Flora McMichael for taking us global. Also, thanks to all in sales, marketing and publicity.

Big cake kisses to super-talented photographer Donal Skehan. I'm so grateful you were able to overcome your fear of not being the star of the show. Look what stunning shots you created for MY book! Seriously, thanks for always being so positive, pushing for the best possible outcome and making my food look amazing when (can you believe?!) it is sometimes not!

Cake and chamomile tea goes to prop stylist Sofie Larsson who brought much-needed Swedish sweetness and calm to the hectic photo shoot, not to mention her gorgeous treasures.

I can't sprinkle enough edible glitter over the kitchen dream team in thanks for the long, hot summer in the *No-Bake Baking* HQ. Thanks to Ajda Mehmet who, when not in a supermarket, was working hard at recipe testing and even harder keeping me sane. Massive thanks also to Emma Nelson, Jette Verdi, Lorna Ni Cheallaigh and Olivia Marjoram.

My no-bake bakes were dressed to the nines with the help of lavish prop loans from **www.avoca.ie**, **www.dunnesstores.com**, **www.articledublin.com** and Louise Dockery, for which I am very grateful. Thanks also to Meta Coyle at **www.decobake.com** for her generous supplies and advice. Hugs and kisses to Claire Ryan at **www.theinformalflorist.com** for her stunning flowers.

A special dusting of icing sugar for all those people who teach, guide, inspire and believe in me along my merry way. In particular, Orla Broderick has held my hand from Day One and I will never outgrow her mentoring. Thanks for being my friend!

My Mam and Dad are the royal icing on the cake. Thanks for instilling a strong work ethic in me and for never doubting my ability to do anything.

The cherry on top goes to my husband Martin (although I know he would much prefer the whole cake). Thanks for never batting an eyelid at the frequent kitchen bombs and prop explosions you come home to. Thanks also for looking after Pearl while I camped out in my cave to write this book. We won't mention her fractured collarbone on the eve of book deadline!

To my little Pearly Pie, it is so cute (and worrying!) that you think my book photos displayed on my office wall are a menu from which to choose your dinner! Nice try. Thanks for being the best person in the world to no-bake bake with!

ABOUT THE AUTHOR

Sharon Hearne-Smith has over 15 years' experience of ghostwriting, recipe testing and food styling for cookbooks, food magazines and TV cookery shows. She has worked with some of the biggest names in the business, including Jamie Oliver, Rachel Allen, Gordon Ramsay, Lorraine Pascale, James Martin and Ina Garten, and on BBC's *Ready Steady Cook*. Sharon lives in Dublin with her husband and young daughter. This is her first solo cookbook.

Quercus Editions Ltd
55 Baker Street
7th Floor, South Block
London
W1U 8EW

First published in 2014

Copyright © Sharon Hearne-Smith, 2014
Photographs © Donal Skehan, 2014

The moral right of Sharon Hearne-Smith to be identified as the author of this work has been asserted in accordance with the Copyright, Design and Patents Act, 1988.

All rights reserved. No part of this publication may be reproduced, stored in a retrieval system, or transmitted in any form or by any means, electronic, mechanical, photocopying, recording, or otherwise, without the prior permission in writing of the copyright owner and publisher.

Quercus Editions Ltd hereby exclude all liability to the extent permitted by law for any errors or omissions in this book and for any loss, damage or expense (whether direct or indirect) suffered by a third party relying on any information contained in this book. Every effort has been made to contact copyright holders. However, the publishers will be glad to rectify in future editions any inadvertent omissions brought to their attention.

A catalogue record of this book is available from the British Library

ISBN 978 1 84866 622 1

Commissioned & edited by Ione Walder
Publishing Director: Jenny Heller
Design: Nicky Barneby
Food styling: Sharon Hearne-Smith
Prop styling: Sofie Larsson & Sharon Hearne-Smith
Copy-editing: Sarah Chatwin

Printed and bound in China

10 9 8 7 6 5 4 3 2 1